THINGS TO DO IN TALLAHASSEE BEFORE YOU DIE

Mickey,
when you return!
enjoy exploring!

12/9/23

100 THINGS TO DO IN TALLAHASSEE BEFORE YOU DIE

• •

ELIZABETH ROSARIO

Reedy Press
PO Box 5131
St. Louis, MO 63139, USA
www.reedypress.com

Library of Congress Control Number: 2023938757

ISBN: 9781681064727

Design by Jill Halpin

Photos by author unless otherwise noted.

Printed in the United States of America
23 24 25 26 27   5 4 3 2

DEDICATION

For my son, Gaby, who loves that I'm always up for an adventure;
my daughter Emma, who low-key loves how I make friends;
and my daughter Nikki, who helped me grow in Tallahassee.

Fish Camp

FISH CAMP
BAIT & TACKLE
CONSUME
ALCOHOLIC BEVERAGES
OPEN CONTAINER
500 FEET
ANY PERSONS
Consuming Beverages
NOT Purchased At
FISH CAMP
WILL BE ASKED TO LEAVE
NO EXCEPTIONS
MEN'S
BATHROOM
OUTDOORS
Tastes Like Heaven,

CONTENTS

Music and Entertainment

Sports and Recreation

Culture and History

J. R. Alford Greenway

ACKNOWLEDGMENTS

Although I am known to go on adventures on my own, I have to thank those of you who were open and sometimes willing participants in my excursions.

My kids often came along with me or gave me the time to discover on my own. My friend Erin Vansickle shared a list of her favorite places. My friend Christie Perkins whose love for this community is shared on the plate of her car helped me with history. Tom Mikota who always said "Let's do it" or "That sounds fun" when I asked him to go on adventures with me. Ebe Randeree is constantly sharing with FSU students what Tallahassee has to offer. Thanks to Sarah Ruggless who is bringing her kids to Tally from Minnesota to experience *100 Things Tallahassee* with me. I am extremely grateful to Juliana Nichols for catching artist Elisa Peña in her element at an outdoor concert in one of Jackson Properties Stadium Houses and to Maddy Reinhart, thank you for making the pictures look beautiful.

Thank you all from the bottom of my heart!

FSU Heritage Tower

PREFACE

My story with Tallahassee goes back to the fall of 1992. I was in ninth grade and living in Puerto Rico. I took a test on all the capitals and states of the United States of America in my social science class. I got 99 percent—I had missed just one. I was upset! I looked down at my paper. I had misspelled one capital. I'd misspelled Tallahassee. A year later, I found myself in the city I had misspelled, the city that kept me from a perfect score. There had to be a reason why.

I moved to Tallahassee on October 31, 1993, and I have lived here ever since. Although it was an adjustment coming from a busy island, I learned to love, appreciate, and understand Tallahassee. I finished my last two years of high school in Tallahassee and attended Florida State University. I have worked for local firms, national companies, and corporate America, and even taught at my alma mater. As the business manager at Jackson Properties, I work within walking distance of FSU Doak Campbell Stadium and I am constantly surrounded by people from all over the states.

I was born and raised in Puerto Rico. I have traveled extensively throughout our nation and, to date, to a dozen other countries, Tallahassee is where I choose to live. I have raised my children here and established networks and a business while creating an oasis near one of my most beloved parks in

Tallahassee. I have grown, discovered, and left a mark on this community, from being the host of Explore Tallahassee for the City of Tallahassee to leaving a permanent finish line downtown while I served as director of the Tallahassee Marathon and Half Marathon. I have been a writing contributor for Visit Tallahassee and *Tallahassee Woman Magazine*, branded the Bannerman Crossings development, was part of Leadership Tallahassee Class 35, was named one of 25 Women You Need to Know in Tallahassee in 2023, and more importantly, I have provided housing for thousands of students that make this community their home during their college years. And Tallahassee has had a tremendous impact on me.

I was tired of people saying "there is nothing to do here," so my friend Rob dared me to find 365 things to do in Tallahassee. In December 2016, I began my quest to create a list of things I love doing in the capital city. Fast-forward to 2022 and the opportunity to write *100 Things to Do in Tallahassee Before You Die* came along, and I am deliriously excited to share my love of this city with the world. Of course, I had no trouble winning the 365 challenge!

Ranked by *Forbes* magazine as one of the top 10 places to live in Florida, selected by HGTV as of the best midsize cities in the United States, and home to one of the top 20 bookstores to visit in Florida as chosen by *Southern Living*, Tallahassee is truly a place where you can constantly find new things to do if you are looking.

You must stay curious, stay active, and let the adventure begin as you explore the capital of Florida, the city of Tallahassee, with me!

It's time to dig for treasures and find the hidden gems!

Proof Brewing Co.

FOOD AND DRINK

1

DINE IN THE HEART OF MIDTOWN
AT BELLA BELLA

Nestled in the center of Tallahassee, Bella Bella has seen the Midtown district grow around it. Tallahassee's best restaurant for homemade fresh Italian fare is decorated by works from local artists, and its colors have a way of making you feel welcome and relaxed as soon as you walk in. You are in a safe space—a place to have conversations, enjoy amazing food, and be part of a family. Whatever you order, make sure you start with their unique and delicious Bubble Bread; truly a must-have. One shouldn't leave without trying at least one of their daily specials, but if you are feeling more traditional, their chicken parmigiana is the way to go. In for just a drink? Step into the Midtown Vino Room, which offers an extensive wine and beer menu, a lounge area, and a second bar to enjoy a night out.

123 E Fifth Ave.
850-412-1114, thebellabella.com

WATCH THE WORLD
AT BLACK DOG CAFE

Surrounded by beautiful and grand oak trees, it is not uncommon to hear people speaking different languages as you sip coffee on Black Dog Cafe's patio while enjoying the view of Lake Ella. Opened by FSU graduate Carla Reid over 22 years ago, Black Dog Cafe has remained a go-to place in the community. It is here that eclectic meets everything else. Enjoy gourmet coffees from all around the world and even craft beer from Proof Brewing Company accompanied by homemade pastries. Step inside an old wooden house with a small play area for kids, dim lighting, and art all over the walls, which offers the tranquility you need to study and the privacy you desire to enjoy a conversation. This is a great place for people-watching that allows the mind to wander and create a new story. On Saturdays, chess players get to test their skills in pickup games with anyone who shows up. Feel free to join them!

229 Lake Ella Dr.
850-224-2518, blackdogcafefl.wixsite.com/blackdogcafe

EXPERIENCE BIG, BOLD, AND FLAVORFUL CRAFT BEER
AT PROOF BREWING COMPANY

In 2012, Angela and Byron Burroughs opened the first craft production beer company in Tallahassee. In 2019, their new city-block-wide location came to life. Proof Brewing is unlike any other brewery in the area, with an impressive 8,000-square-foot beer garden, a covered patio, a private event space, a restaurant, a tasting room, and contemporary decor. You will never want to leave. Proof also has live music every evening, Thursday through Sunday. Located within walking distance of Cascades Park, the historical community of Myers Park, and the SOMO district of Tallahassee, Proof is the perfect place to enjoy an entire afternoon with live music, a trivia night, a game watch party, or even a dancing class while drinking their popular Mango Witbier or EightFive-O pale ale. Don't leave without touring their brewing room where 30,000 barrels a year are crafted and distributed.

1320 S Monroe St.
850-577-0517, proofbrewingco.com

TIP

Our local brewery scene has grown! Celebrate with us yearly at the Tallahassee Beer Festival to sample beers from over 100 home brewers and breweries. Check out their website for more info: tlhbeerfest.com

CHECK OUT THESE LOCAL BREWERIES

Lake Tribe
3357 Garber Dr., #4
laketribebrewing.com

Deep Brewing
2524 Cathat Ct., #2
850-567-0295, deepbrewing.com

Oyster City Brewing
603 W Gaines St., Suite 7
850-629-4518, oystercity.beer

Amicus Brewing Ventures
717 S Gadsden St.
amicusbrewingventures.com

Fools Fire Brewing
415 Saint Francis St., Unit 112
850-727-4033, facebook.com/foolsfirebrew

Ology Brewing
118 E Sixth Ave.
850-296-2809, ologybrewing.com

For a complete list of craft breweries,
visit tlhbeers.com

BRUNCH WITH JERI

AT JERI'S CAFE IN MIDTOWN

She is fun, energetic, and filled with joy! It's simply Jeri! Her energy is contagious and she will be part of your family as soon as you step into her world. Tucked away in midtown under the Midtown Reader bookstore and behind a park, a fun experience awaits. The atmosphere is filled with charm. Choose to dine on their darling and delightfully designed outside patio or step inside for the best breakfast/lunch in town. With homestyle dishes you won't find at home, Jeri's brings farm-to-table cuisine to life with rich, authentic, and robust flavors combined by their creative chef. It is all about having exceptional experiences with the foods you love. Jeri's serves the best lobster bisque you have ever had and makes the best sandwiches in town. While you wait you will fall in love with the complimentary pimento cheese and don't be afraid to ask for more.

1123 Thomasville Rd.
850-385-7268, jerismidtowncafe.com

TIP

Head upstairs and stroll through our local bookstore, Midtown Reader, or have a cup of coffee from Piebrary Coffee. Want to walk off your lunch instead? Cross the street and head on over to Lafayette Park for an enjoyable walk in one of Tallahassee's favorite neighborhoods.

5

PUT A CUBAN IN YOUR MOUTH
AT GORDOS

Walk in to the rhythmic sounds of Spanish music, a lively atmosphere with beach-theme decor, and a large deck that welcomes you to Gordos, where it all started on Pensacola Street. Called by some "The Jackpot of Cuban Food," Gordos founder Eddie Agramonte brought Hialeah to Tallahassee in 1988 using his mom's recipes. The menu includes all the Cuban classics from croquetas and *picadillo* to wraps and burgers to satisfy everyone's *antojitos*. You must try the grilled chicken with black beans and rice, and don't forget to get those *tostones* on the side. With two locations in town, one for the college community in Pensacola Street and another for the family community in Market Square, Eddie continues to provide access to excellent Cuban food in Tallahassee. Don't leave without your own Gordos's cup filled with a SMASH, their signature rum punch. This Cuban is here to stay!

1907 W Pensacola St.
850-576-5767

1460 Market St., Ste. 3–4
850-727-5914, gordoscubanfood.com

6

EAT, DRINK, AND TALK LOUD
AT KOOL BEANZ CAFE

The *New York Times* described Kool Beanz as a "great little restaurant," which is celebrating over 25 years in Tallahassee. Originally from London, owner/chef Keith Baxter has lived and traveled all over the world and brought his eclectic experience to Tallahassee. Bright colors, modern art, and the constant chatter of people make this place fun and welcoming. Enjoy dining inside or on a covered patio but know that the best seat in the house is by the bar, where you can rejoice in seeing how the food is made right in front of your eyes.

Kool Beanz offers a menu that changes daily with fascinating starters, greens, and salads; delicious entrées including an ever-present mojo chicken, shrimp, chorizo, black beans, rice, and pepper-jack cheese; and a rich variety of desserts by Sylvia Gould, a James Beard Award nominee.

Kool Beanz is an amazing, eclectic, and not-so-small, hole-in-the-wall place with excellent food and service.

Here you are among friends!

921 Thomasville Rd.
850-224-2466, koolbeanz-cafe.com

TAKE A DETOUR
AT WOODCHUCK'S CAFE

If the GPS leads you to a gas station, don't panic: just know that if you see neon green, you have arrived at your destination. Out of the way, near a residential area, and known only by locals, Woodchuck's opened its doors on May 20, 2013. This is where hungry people come to be happy! Chris Benfield, a native of Tallahassee, has been cooking his famous homestyle food for almost 20 years.

Open only for breakfast and lunch, Woodchuck's provides an extensive menu of dishes made with fresh ingredients that will keep you coming back for more. It's time to try steak and eggs for breakfast, sweet potato pancakes, the Dead Texan, or the Godzilla burger for lunch. Great service, fair prices, flavorful meals, and friendly staff awaits!

2520 W Tharpe St.
850-224-9766, woodchucks-cafe.com

8

GET INTIMATE

AT MIMI'S TABLE BISTRO AND WINE BAR

Don't let the small space fool you! At Mimi's you are in for a great, flavorful, and exquisite experience at the hands of owner and executive chef William Lawson. Located in the Old Town neighborhood of Tallahassee, Mimi's Table has become a favorite place to enjoy a great meal and a good glass of wine. European technique and cuisine meet southern roots to create an exceptional dining experience where a quiet, reserved, and open setting with attentive staff welcomes you. Simple yet flavorful ingredients are used to craft every meal. Make sure to try the chef's sample special of the day and know the best seat in the house is by the window. Stay on the lookout for their coveted monthly Chef's Meals, a private, multi-course, chef-prepared dinner and wine pairing, and enjoy an evening all to yourself.

1311 Miccosukee Rd.
850-999-8406, mimistabletally.com

9

ENJOY THE GAME
AT MADISON SOCIAL

It's simply the vibe! Founded by two FSU alumni, Brian McKenna and Matt Thompson, Madison Social opened its garage doors on August 31, 2013, to show Tally how to have a great time. As the front-and-center restaurant of College Town, Madison Social has the perfect view of FSU Doak S. Campbell Stadium. Enjoy their award-winning BLT dip and the popular MadSo burger topped with fried avocado, maple-pepper bacon, aged cheddar, whiskey caramelized onion, and a rosemary aioli alongside a beer from their extensive selection. The Sunday brunch menu with mimosas is a must after an FSU football game or a night out on the town. Want to hang out a little longer? Watch as MadSo turns into a bar after 9 p.m. and enjoy their specialty cocktail, the Madison Mule. Be sure to check out their website for their merch and ask about the storyteller shirt of Airport Drive.

705 S Woodward Ave.
850-894-6276, madisonsocial.com

10

PARTY LIKE IT'S 1965
AT WATERWORKS

It's time to forget your troubles, escape the grind of modern life, and get together at Tallahassee's only 1960s-style premier tiki bar and restaurant where stories come to life to be retold for years to come. Not your average bar, Waterworks is filled with bamboo fixtures, carved tiki heads, and unforgettable water windows (hence the name). This place has been a social and cultural landmark for almost 30 years. From old-school-style cooking and more than 50 drinks you won't find anywhere else to educational speakers, live music, dance performances, and theme nights, Waterworks is a place where even award-winning directors and actors have found joy. Owner Don Quarello takes great pleasure in giving locals a place of their own. The Waterworks patio serves as an afternoon sanctuary for musicians, artists, writers, and those who simply want to go back in time.

1133 Thomasville Rd.
850-224-1887, tikitallahassee.com

11

DRINK WITH HISTORY
AT BAR 1903

There is nothing more unique than to be surrounded by history. Originally named after Florida's eighth governor, the David S. Walker Library (also known as the University Library) was Tallahassee's first library, constructed in 1903, hence the reference to the date in its current name. In 1976, the building was listed in the National Register of Historic Places, reflecting the early 20th-century architecture and the history of education in Tallahassee. Its historic brick front with large columns remains, and once you step inside you are immediately transported back in time; from the floors to the original oil lamps, you are living history. Its impressive cocktail menu is divided into periods and spans over 160 years. Pair a historic cocktail with great food. You simply can't go wrong with the artisan cheese board, the grilled buffalo chicken sandwich, or the burrata antipasto. Seating is limited and coveted.

A library of cocktails awaits!

209 E Park Ave.
850-354-9739, bar1903tlh.com

TIP

If you have to wait, enjoy a stroll around the Chain of Parks right across the street on Park Avenue, ending by Old City Cemetery.

12

UNWIND AND ENJOY THE VIEW AT CHARLIE PARK

An engaging space with gorgeous panoramic views, picturesque house-made cocktails, and nonstop tapas—need I say more? As soon as you walk into Charlie Park, you know this is where happy hour was reimagined for Tallahassee. Located on the rooftop of the AC Hotel by Marriott and overlooking Cascade Park, the Capital Cascade Connector Bridge, and the SOMO district, Charlie Park's elevator doors open to a comfortable and sophisticated setting ready to be enjoyed with your friends. Sit on the terrace for stunning sunset views with their signature cocktail, the Charlie, on hand and a maple slab bacon small plate that speaks for itself. With a unique ambiance and one of the most extensive wine lists found anywhere in the city, Charlie Park is the perfect place for happy hour, special events, and even their ultimate grazing brunch—all on the rooftop.

801 S Gadsden St.
850-759-4300, charlieparkrooftop.com

HIT ALL THE ROOF TOP BARS

Level 8 Lounge
415 N Monroe St.
850-224-6000

Eve on Adams
101 S Adam St.
850-521-6018, eoatally.com

Recess at College Town
705 S Woodward Ave.
850-570-8535, therecessclub.com

13

DRINK GREAT COFFEE
AT RED EYE COFFEE

Red Eye Coffee started in the heart of Midtown and quickly became one of Tallahassee's favorite gathering coffee places. Frequented by local business owners, business professionals, politicians and non-profit leaders in our community, Red Eye Coffe is the perfect place to have a comfortable meeting, host an event and even hold political forums while enjoying great and locally roasted coffee.

In 2022, Barbo Moro, a Cuban-American stepped into the owner role at Red Eye Coffee with a focus on giving back to the community. The only Latina-owned coffee shop in Tallahassee, Red Eye Coffee offers more than just great coffee. Regional gift sets, shareables menu, charcurreie boards and beer and wine can be enjoyed at their Midtown location for Happy Hour with your choice of indoor or outdoor seating.

With two locations in the capital city, Red Eye Coffee is dedicated to sustainability and a positive impact in Tallahassee.

RedEye: Midtown
1122 Thomasville Rd.
850-425-5701

RedEye: Capital Circle
1196 Capital Cir. NE, Unit D
850-999-8278

redeyecoffee.com

STOP INTO THESE COFFEE SHOPS

Tally is a midsize community
with a big-city love for caffeine.

Lucky Goat Coffee
luckygoatcoffee.com

Catalina Cafe
facebook.com/catalinacafetally

The Sweet Shop
facebook.com/sweetshoplounge

Power Plant Cafe
edisontally.com/cafe

Vino Beano
vinobeano.com

Square Mug Café
squaremugcafe.wixsite.com/squaremugcafe

Tally Cat Café
tallycatcafe.com

La Florida Coffee and Wine
lafloridacoffeewine.com

Paper Fox Coffee
paperfoxcoffee.com

The Piebrary
midtownreader.com

Grounds OPS Roastery and Bakehouse
groundopscoffee.com

EAT BREAKFAST
AT CANOPY ROAD CAFÉ

Because every great southern town needs an even greater place for breakfast, welcome to Canopy Road Café, named after Tallahassee's beautiful and scenic canopy roads. Peanut butter and banana pancakes filled with chopped bacon and topped with peanut butter drizzle . . . meet the Elvis pancakes. Croissant French toast, cinnamon rolls, churro waffles, need I say more? If you are in for lunch, don't second-guess it—just order their cinnamon roll burger. It's an addictive dare!

Tallahassee is lucky to have four different locations, but it all began on 1913 Monroe Street. FSU alumni Brad Buckenheimer and David Raney opened Canopy Road in 2007 and have never looked back. Canopy Road has locations in Jacksonville, Tampa, and Rosemary Beach!

Take home their house-made Canopy Road hot sauce and the Lucky Goat Canopy Road coffee blend.

1913 N Monroe St.
850-668-6600

2202 Capital Cir. NE
850-893-0466

3196 Merchants Row Blvd.
850-329-2827

1779 Apalachee Pkwy.
850-727-0263

111 Old Water Oak Rd.
Opening Spring 2023

canopyroadcafe.com

VISIT SOME GREAT BREAKFAST SPOTS

Jeri's Love on a Plate
1370 Market St., Ste. 1
50-756-7660, jerismidtowncafe.com

The Bada Bean
2500 Apalachee Pkwy., Ste. B
850-562-2326, thebadabean.com

The Lunchbox
295 N Magnolia Dr.
850-942-9766, lunchboxtally.com

Country Kitchen
3840 N Monroe St., #105
850-562-3293, facebook.com/people/
country-kitchen/100063877800012

15

EXPERIENCE THE EFFECT
AT BLU HALO

Tallahassee native Keith Paniucki had a vision of providing Tallahassee with a culinary experience like no other, and Blu Halo has, without a doubt, elevated the capital city's cuisine to another level. Drive to Bannerman Crossings and you will forget that you are surrounded by oak trees and canopy roads as you step into an upscale world under the neon halo. Take a moment to admire the exquisite open setting filled with contemporary yet warm decor and a lavish tower of liquors surrounded by an upscale martini bar where there is a private room on the side. Step out to their covered patio, simply perfect for movie and concert nights at the Bannerman Pavilion, and don't miss out on the best brunch north of I-10. It's time to splurge, so bring good company and enjoy the lively atmosphere, terrific food, delicious and exclusive martinis, and exemplary service that Blu Halo will provide.

3431 Bannerman Rd., Ste. 102
850-999-1696, thebluhalo.com

16

EXPERIMENT WITH BEER

AT OLOGY BREWING

With a dad who studied olfaction, a grandpa researching taste and sense, and a decade of science experiments with beer combined with a biology degree, owner Nick Walter is extremely qualified to make beer. Encouraged by a love for craft beer and science, Walter opened Ology's doors in the Summer of 2017 in Midtown and has not stopped experimenting with new libations ever since. From its three Tallahassee locations to statewide distribution and even a new taproom in Tampa, Ology Brewing is here to shake things up! Unexplored waters have even entered our capital city as Ology becomes the first distillery in the area serving potato vodka and rum. Whether you head over to their cozy Midtown location where even coffee is brewed, their grand patio on Powell Mill for an evening of fun, or their spacious Northside location to bring all your friends, Ology is the place to be!

118 E 6th Ave.
850-296-2809

2708 Power Mill Ct., Ste. A
850-296-2809

2910 Kerry Forest Parkway, Unit 8
850-296-2809

ologybrewing.com

TIP

The Power Mill location is adjacent to Tom Brown Park. Bring your bike, tackle the trails, and finish with a Sensory Overload IPA on hand!

EAT A BIG SLICE
AT MOMO'S PIZZA

If you are looking for a casual place that serves slices as big as your head, only Momo's Pizza fits that description. In 1999, Don Dye started Momo's right across from FSU's campus on Tennessee Street with an authentic New York–style pizza recipe. It was a hole in the wall, peculiar yet with unique personality, and the food was reasonably priced. Great crust and tasty pepperoni make it a delicious pizza. The calzones are big enough to share, and if you order a large pie to go, make sure your car is big enough to fit the giant box. Momo's now has three locations, each with a unique appeal, the same tasty food, and a varied beer collection. Its Tennessee Street location is perfect if you are looking for eclectic. Market Street is great to enjoy a day out on the porch, and Pensacola has a more traditional feel.

1416 W Tennessee St.
850-224-9808

1410 Market St.
850-412-0222

1641 Pensacola St.
850-900-5784

momospizza.com

DISCOVER SAGE

An intimate and comfortable atmosphere, attentive service, and delicious food make an evening at Sage restaurant unforgettable. Owner and chef Terry White was named one of the nation's best chefs by the inaugural edition of *Best Chefs America,* and Sage has been a staple in Tallahassee for almost 20 years. This neighborhood restaurant is located in the beloved Market District and offers American cuisine with a sophisticated and worldly vibe. Choose from a selection of small bites such as the bar steak *frites*. Indulge in pecan-crusted mahi mahi or their Idaho red trout, and completely spoil yourself with their seasonal desserts, the extensive wine list, or a must-try list of house cocktails.

Walk into a casual setting and be ready to try delicately prepared meals made with fresh local produce while having a unique multicultural experience.

3534 Maclay Blvd. S
850-270-9396, sagetallahassee.com

19

TASTE DIVERSITY
IN THE CAPITAL CITY

Not that long ago, Tallahassee was seen as a place lacking in diverse cuisine. Today, Tally has grown into a mini cultural mecca where you can dine on food from all over the world. There is enough diversity so that locals can have the luxury of trying something new every month, yet if you have only a short time in Tallahassee, don't leave without trying a few of our favorites:

Essence of India—Traditional Indian dishes with flavorful spices and vegetarian options.

Sahara Greek and Lebanese Cafe—Mama Sophia has been cooking her Middle Eastern recipes in Tallahassee for over 20 years with a Mediterranean twist.

Café de Martin—The perfect place to taste the love of Lima, Peru, either indoors or on a secluded patio with live music on some Fridays.

Pitaria—Serving classic Greek food in Tallahassee since 1991, where you order over the counter.

Azu—This is where 40 years of experience cooking Chinese, Japanese, sushi, and Asian fusion cuisine come together in Tallahassee.

San Miguel Mexican Restaurant—Ranchero style setting created by Coahuila, Mexico native Felipe Reinosa has been serving Tally since 1995.

TAKE YOUR TASTE BUDS AROUND THE WORLD

Essence of India
1105 Apalachee Pkwy., Ste. A
850-656-7200, essenceofindiafl.com

Sahara Greek and Lebanese Restaurant
1135 Apalachee Pkwy.
850-656-1800, saharacafeone.com

Café De Martin
2743 Capital Cir. NE
850-900-5969, cafedemartin.com

Pitaria
1935 Apalachee Pkwy.
850-765-1171, thepitaria.com

Azu Lucy Ho's Restaurant
3220 Apalachee Pkwy., #13
850-893-4112, azulucyhos.com

San Miguel Mexican Restaurant
200 W Tharpe St.
850-385-3346, sanmiguelmexicanrestaurant.weebly.com

SEARCH FOR PARADISE
AT PINEAPPÉTIT

Proof that Tallahassee's food culture is vibrant and growing can be found at Pineappétit. What started as a catering company evolved in 2018 into a food truck venture that allowed Tallahassee to experience the soulful flavors of the Caribbean. Chef Sam Burgess, a graduate of Florida Agricultural and Mechanical University (FAMU), fell in love with the taste of Caribbean, Jamaican, and Haitian food when he moved to Florida. He now shares this love with the community in Tallahassee. Everything on his menu is delicious, but you simply must try a pineapple bowl, consisting of a pineapple cut in half and filled with rice and your choice of protein and topped with a signature salsa. It is an Instagram-worthy dish you will want to order again and again. In 2021, after three years of being chased down on his food truck, Chef Sam opened a brick-and-mortar restaurant with seating for customers to enjoy paradise in a casual atmosphere.

2037 W Pensacola St.
850-354-8242, pineappetit.com

Track Food Truck Locations
instagram.com/pineappetittally
facebook.com/pineappetittally

21

LET THE GOOD TIMES POUR
AT GROWLER COUNTRY

There is one place where it is easy to make friends, watch a game, order a drink, and let the good times pour; it is Growler Country. Florida's first dedicated growler filling station recently celebrated a decade in Tallahassee. With its laid-back, friendly atmosphere and tasty food, you are sure to have a good time. Choose from an impressive, rotating selection of 41 select craft beers ranging from local brews to exceptional and rare brews from all over the country. Create a match made in heaven when you pair beer with some of their hot buttered pretzels, two-dollar tacos, or a foot-long hot dog topped with mac and cheese, bacon, green onion, and sriracha drizzle. Test your aim in darts or play Skee-Ball and fill up your growler. This is where the good times pour.

3305 Capital Cir. NE
850-765-7771, growlercountry.com

22

INDULGE IN SWEETNESS
AT TALLAHASSEE BAKERIES

Tasty Pastry Bakery

The Cross family is responsible for making people happy in Tallahassee for the past 60 years. Tasty Pastry Bakery is in the Market District and bakes the best bread, cookies, cakes, and pies while also serving dinner casseroles to make the family night easier.

1355 Market St., Ste. A5

850-893-3752, tastypastrybakery.com

Au Péché Mignon

Open a window into the most elegant, exquisite, and sinful collection of European pastries in the capital city. For 24 years, Au Péché Mignon has provided delicious macaroons, chocolate, cheese, and lunch sandwiches in downtown Tallahassee.

220 N Duval St.
850-668-5533, frenchpastrytallahassee.com

Treva's Pastries & Fine Foods

Grab and go or enjoy the ambiance of a bistro-style pastry shop and café. Find a little bit of everything: dinner plates, sandwiches with freshly baked bread, croissants, specialty cakes, and yummy pastries at Treva's Pastries. Serving Tallahassee for 10 years!

2766 Capital Cir. NE
850-765-0811, trevas.net

ENJOY THESE LOCAL EATERIES

Clusters and Hops
1866 Thomasville Rd.
winencheese.com

Dao
3425 Bannerman Rd.
Unit A102
850-999-1482
daotally.com

Food Glorious Food
1950 Thomasville Rd.
Ste. C
850-224-9974
food-glorious-food.
squarespace.com

Georgio's Fine Food and Spirits
2971 Apalachee Pkwy.
850-877-3211
georgiostallahassee.com

Il Lusso
201 E Park Ave.,
Ste. 100
850-765-8620
illussotally.com

Riccardo's Restaurant
1950 Thomasville Rd.
850-386-3988
riccardostally.com

Savour
115 E Park Ave.
850-765-6966
savourtallahassee.com

Table 23
1215 Thomasville Rd.
850-329-2261
table23tally.com

Z. Bardhi's
3596 Kinhega Dr.
850-894-9919
zbardhis.com

Leola's Crab Shack
2110 S Adams St.
850-575-0395
leolastallahassee.com/32315

Little Paris Tallahassee
1355 Market St.
850-765-7457
littleparistallahassee.com

The Huntsman
320 E Tennessee St.
850-765-1887, huntsmantallahassee.com

For a complete list of restaurants in the capital city,
visit tallahasseefoodies.com

Elisa Peña on stage at a Jackson Properties Stadium House

MUSIC AND ENTERTAINMENT

23

BRUNCH, READ, AND BREW ALL UNDER ONE ROOF

AT MIDTOWN READER, PIEBRARY, AND JERI'S CAFE

She had a dream, a stack of books, and a very comfy chair. In November 2016, Sally Bradshaw opened Midtown Reader as Tallahassee's only *New York Times*–reporting, independent bookstore, selling new books. It's the perfect place to find your next good read. Walk under the painted tree as you enter the children's cove and don't miss out on our Florida authors and books highlighting Florida's political, social, and natural history. There is something for everyone in this magical building. Start downstairs at Jeri's Midtown Cafe, where brunch is a must. Make your way upstairs to find your brew at the Piebrary while reading and meeting new people. The front-porch seating provides the perfect space for enjoying your new book with your furry friend. From author events to Kidtown Story Time and book clubs to workshops and even open mic nights, Midtown Reader has it all.

1123 Thomasville Rd.
850-425-2665, midtownreader.com

24

GET INSPIRED AT OPENING NIGHTS

AT FLORIDA STATE UNIVERSITY

What started as a seven-day festival in February of 1999 under FSU President Sandy D'Alemberte has turned into an annual series of performances that engage students, locals, and surrounding communities and expose them to world-renowned music, dance, theater, visual art, film, and spoken word. Opening Nights aims to provide free educational opportunities for students by introducing them to visiting artists and performers. Yet there are no words to describe the talent that comes to perform at Florida State University. Patti Labelle, Jay Leno, Mykal Kilgore, Dance Theatre of Harlem, the Wayne Shorter Quartet, and Jerry Seinfeld, among hundreds of others, have all set foot on their stages, and the list continues to grow and impress us. Many of the performances take place in their grand Ruby Diamond Auditorium and their smaller stages provide an intimate experience unlike any other.

These are performances you simply cannot miss!

openingnights.fsu.edu

25

PLAY POOL
AT THE PALACE SALOON

Whether you are starting or ending your night, all roads lead to the Palace Saloon. Established by Chuck Fisher in 1972 and sold to Lora and Russ Lowe in 2008, the Palace is a staple of Tallahassee football tradition. Located just steps away from FSU Doak Campbell Stadium, patrons can walk, hop, or stampede in for some good old-fashioned fun! It's all about pitchers of beer, pool tables, darts, arcade games, their famous sake shots, and all-day tailgating on FSU game days. It's Tallahassee's favorite smoky dive bar. This is a place where you pick the music and memorable moments are stored for generations to come. No need to dress up. The Palace Saloon has the most relaxed setting in town. Come in ready to be surprised and have a good time!

The Palace Saloon is a place you can call home. It's not just a bar; it's a family reunion!

1303 Jackson Bluff Rd.
850-575-3418, palacesaloontally.com

TIP

Don't miss the Gulf Winds Track Club Palace Saloon 5K every April with nonstop free beer and live music after your run.

SEE THE HOLIDAY LIGHTS
AT DOROTHY B. OVEN PARK

A manor home designed and built in the 1930s by Dr. Alfred Maclay, where the Camellia Nursery built by Breckenridge Gamble once stood, and donated to the City of Tallahassee in 1985 by Will J. Oven Jr. solely to be used as a city park, Dorothy B. Oven Park is truly a hidden gem. Filled with history, loved by locals, and unknown to the outside world are over six acres of lush gardens nestled under ancient live oaks and filled with trails, ponds, splendid azaleas, camellias, and local flora not found elsewhere. During the Christmas season, the gardens turn into a magnificent display of over 250,000 lights, holiday music, moving displays, warm treats, and even Santa and his helpers, who make a magical appearance on the third Thursday in December in a 20-year tradition called Elf Night. The manor retains its historic charm and is used for special events year-round.

3205 Thomasville Rd.
850-891-3915, talgov.com/parks/centers-oven

TIP

Don't miss the splendid camellia gardens in full bloom during February and mid-March.

EXPERIENCE THE JOY
AT WORD OF SOUTH

One of the greatest literary and music festivals in America, founded by former city commissioner and author Mark Mustian, Word of South is a weekend devoted to arts and culture. It is a unique festival where authors join musicians to bring their sounds to the world and sometimes to trade places. Since its inaugural weekend in 2015, Word of South has seen performances by musical legends, award-winning authors, and musicians such as Jamey Johnson, Ben Folds, Cynthia Barnett, and even Roy McCurdy; the list is immense. With over 100 artists performing at the festival each year, every genre of music and literature can be experienced in the beauty of Tallahassee spring at Cascade Park. Children also enjoy a formidable program that encourages a love for books and music, and selected performances are on Livestream to be enjoyed wherever you are.

1001 S Gadsden St.
wordofsouthfestival.com

TIP

Want to experience more? Walk over the Cascade Connector Bridge into Proof Brewing Company for a cold draft. Head upstairs to Charlie Park to see the action from above, eat at the Edison while listening to the music, or simply drive through the historic community of Myers Park on your way out.

HAVE A BOTTOMLESS DRINK
AT BULLWINKLE'S SALOON

Bullwinkle's, known to many as just Bull's is the infamous place where all college students come to celebrate their 21st birthdays. Located right across from Florida State University and on the notorious Tennessee "Strip" since 1979, Bullwinkle's will give you a night that unfortunately you may soon forget. Walk into a true, old-school-style saloon famous for its $10 Bottomless Buffet with TopShelf Liquor and the right for passage with your Moose monthly membership. Hang outside and people-watch from the top of the double-decker porch or get rowdy with the DJ down below at the beer garden. Let your hair down, put on your cowboy hat and boots, and enjoy the southern ranch vibe with some good ol' whiskey in your hand! It's time to have a good time at Bullwinkle's tonight!

620 W Tennessee St.
850-224-0651, bullwinklessaloon.com

29

STROLL THROUGH THE ART
AT LEMOYNE'S CHAIN OF PARKS ART FESTIVAL

Ranked as the number one Florida art festival and seventh-best art festival nationwide in the fine art and design category by *Sunshine Artist* magazine, LeMoyne's Chain of Parks Art Festival is a cultural gem in our community. With over 100 artists' booths nestled under majestic oak trees, this multiday fine arts festival has something for everyone. Great weather, live music stages located in the heart of the festival, food trucks, kids' corners, and even 3D chalk-walk artists add to the experience for a weekend you will never forget. Meet the artists and learn why they do what they do! This fun-filled and high-quality art festival brings artists from all across the nation and over 40,000 visitors and instills a never-ending love for our capital city in all of them. Stay long enough or come back to enjoy the Saturday Evening Groove in the Chain of Parks.

Come to fall in love with Tallahassee!

125 N Gadsden St.
850-222-8800, chainofparks.org

WATCH THE SHOW
AT THEATRE TALLAHASSEE

Situated on over three acres in the heart of Betton Hills on Thomasville Road since 1961, the Tallahassee Little Theatre was founded in February 1949. The name was formally changed to Theatre Tallahassee in August 2013 to provide a vision for the future. The lobby, named the Magnolia Room, gives way to a cozy space and canteen area to socialize in before and after the show. Walk into the Studio, a black-box-style performance space, and you will immediately experience the warmth and intimate feel of the room. It is here where you can allow vulnerability to enter your world. The shows performed in this space will evoke understanding, empathy, and oftentimes tears. It is a sacred place created to include everyone. The main stage allows for a 360-degree experience you will never forget. Soak up 70 years of history in a world made to entertain, educate, and transform.

1861 Thomasville Rd.
850-224-8474, theatretallahassee.org

TIPS

Looking for a more family-friendly venue? Visit Tallahassee Young Actors Theatre, where graduates include Cheryl Hines, Tony Hall, and Allison Miller.

youngactorstheatre.com

For a 360-degree live experience visit Tallahassee Wanderlust, a theater on location.

facebook.com/wanderlustonlocation

31

CELEBRATE OUR CAPITAL'S HISTORY

AT SPRINGTIME TALLAHASSEE

Designated one of the top festivals in the Southeast, Springtime Tallahassee began in 1968 as the result of a legislative effort to keep Tallahassee as the state capital. Springtime Tallahassee is an exclusive opportunity to showcase our capital city and a chance to go back in time. The festival kicks off with a Friday night music festival on Kleeman Plaza with nationally renowned musicians. The Grand Parade, one of the city's most beloved events, showcases more than 100 dance groups and elaborate floats representing over 400 years of history with krewes from the Spanish-American, Territory, and Statehood Wars; Reconstruction; and the 20th century. A must-see parade with horse-drawn carriages and the magnificent FAMU Marching 100 Band energizes the streets. The jubilee at the downtown Chain of Parks offers music, food, and arts and crafts from all over the country with something for everyone.

Bring your costumes and have a good time!

springtimetallahassee.com

TIP

Before the parade, and only steps away from downtown near Cascades Park, join the Gulf Winds Track Club and run the beloved, challenging, and fun Springtime 10K with one-mile and 5K options.

TIP

While at Kleeman Plaza for the music festival, step over and rejoice over the Tallahassee Marathon and Half Marathon finish line, a memento of the collaboration among the City of Tallahassee, then-marathon director Ely Rosario, and Gulf Winds Track Club. It is one of the only permanent finish lines in the USA. #owntally

GAZE AT THE STARS
AT MOON OVER MACLAY

Truly an exquisite and magical evening as you watch the full moon rise over Lake Hall, the Moon over Maclay concert brings internationally acclaimed jazz musicians and our entertaining local favorites to enchant us in the heart of one of Tallahassee's most beautiful places, Maclay Gardens State Park. Walk down a cobblestone path lit with candles as you enter an enchanting world under the stars. Watch as artists perform on the porch of the Maclay House surrounded by ancient oak trees covered with Spanish moss. Bring your blanket, picnic table or chairs, and the drinks and snacks of your choice, and choose your place on the lawn. For over a decade, Moon over Maclay has provided a spectacular setting where you can relax and enjoy amazing music only known to a few.

It will take your breath away!

Presented by Friends of Maclay Gardens
3540 Thomasville Rd.
850-487-4556, friendsofmaclaygardens.org

LISTEN TO THE MUSIC
AT TALLAHASSEE SYMPHONY ORCHESTRA

In 1979, a noted violinist named Nicholas Harsanyi gifted the world with exceptional live symphony music when he founded the Tallahassee Symphony Orchestra. Director Darko Butorak, who entered his 10th and final season in 2023–24, permeates each performance with incredible passion. Every concert provides a high-level musical experience at the visually stunning Ruby Diamond Auditorium at Florida State University during their five-masterpiece series. The remaining season comprises community partnerships such as Opening Nights, Word of South, and the City of Tallahassee to showcase the capital city's natural and mesmerizing beauty in outdoor concerts. Surround yourself with extraordinary music, get inspired, and enjoy the Tallahassee Symphony Orchestra in the Capital City Amphitheatre at the Halloween Spooktacular, overlooking Central Park Lake under a clear night sky for Pops in the Park at Southwood, dropping into one of their free open rehearsals, or live-steaming a performance in the comfort of your home. Their mission is to make music accessible to all!

515 E Park Ave.
850-224-0461, tallahasseesymphony.org

CATCH A GOLDEN TRADITION
AT THE FSU FLYING HIGH CIRCUS

Seventy-five years of flying high! Founded as an effort for men and women to participate jointly after FSU became a coed institution, the FSU Flying High Circus will take your breath away. The circus has performed in Europe, Canada, the Bahamas, and the West Indies, but it has its permanent home in Tallahassee. The FSU Flying High Circus is the only collegiate circus in the state of Florida and the only one in the nation with a big-top tent. These agile FSU students share an obvious bond as they defy gravity and competently catch each other in midair, providing their audiences with the experience of a lifetime. Grace, power, and determination are all brought together in an unmatched golden tradition. Be sure to witness some of their jaw-dropping routines throughout their home show series; their Halloween show is not to be missed. It's time to run away and join the circus!

In the spring of 1974, several members of the circus pranked the campus by streaking on Landis Green. Hey! It was the '70s!

269 Chieftan Way
850-644-4874, circus.fsu.edu

PLIÉ OR SAUTÉ
AT TALLAHASSEE BALLET

Never did founder Helen Salter think the Tallahassee Ballet would be celebrating 50 years of continuous performance in the capital city! The ballet had humble beginnings, practicing in the lower levels of a mall. Then it moved into a non-air-conditioned room in what now is the Governors Club. From there they commandeered unused rooms in a library only to scavenge dance space in several other locations throughout the years. Today, the male dancers and ballerinas proudly occupy a state-of-the-art, 14,000-square-foot facility. The Tallahassee Ballet continues to unite the people in this community with its great mix of dancers of all ages and abilities, including professionals who engage audiences with their performances of classical and contemporary ballet. Their season opens in September with three performances a year, including the Christmas favorite, *The Nutcracker*, performed to live music at the Ruby Diamond Concert Hall. You will be fully captivated and impressed by the talent, passion, and love these lithe dancers display.

2910 Kerry Forest Pkwy., Ste. C1
850-224-6917, tallahasseeballet.org

TIP

Another local ballet performance center is Pas de Vie Ballet.

pasdevieballet.com/home-pdv

CHILL OUT
AT FISH CAMP AT LAKE IAMONIA

It's a bit of a drive, and you may start to think you are in the middle of nowhere because there is nothing in sight. Yet, you will know when you arrive. A dirt parking lot, an alluring view of the lake, and live music will greet you. Welcome to Fish Camp! With a spacious outdoor area filled with colorful picnic tables, firepits in between, and a vibrant wooden building with a wrap-around deck overlooking the lake, another place like Fish Camp cannot be found anywhere else in Tallahassee. This is a true North Florida hangout frequented only by locals—a hidden treasure with a casual, inviting atmosphere and an unbelievable view. Grab any open seat, order your food and drinks, and get ready to disconnect while you chill and listen to live music overlooking the beautiful Lake Iamonia.

12062 Waterfront Dr.
850-228-7115, fish-camp-at-lake-iamonia.business.site

TIP

Stay to watch the sunset; it's a view you will never forget. Want to make it an adventure? Bring your boat, kayak, paddleboard, or canoe with you, enjoy the water, and stay to eat, drink, and listen to music all afternoon.

LAUNCH INTO SPACE
AT THE CHALLENGER LEARNING CENTER OF TALLAHASSEE

It is time to explore, learn, and entertain yourself at the Challenger Learning Center. Conveniently located in downtown Tallahassee, the Challenger Learning Center opened its doors in 2003 to provide a regional hub to help future generations find a love and passion for science, technology, engineering, and mathematics (STEM). With 32,000 square feet of education programming, interactive facilities, and even Hollywood films, the Challenger has a space mission simulator, IMAX 3D theater, a dome theater, and a planetarium. You don't have to be a kid or a space geek to fall in love with the Challenger. Rich and relevant cultural experiences are provided through documentaries, international movies, and guest speakers to expand your knowledge and spark your curiosity. Kids will be mesmerized by the Challenger's rich programming including SCI Saturdays and day/summer camps. Mark your calendar for free kids' days for hands-on activities and a movie.

200 S Duval St.
850-645-7796, challengertlh.com

DANCE
AT STUDIO D

It is time to move your hips, feel the music, and dance with friends at Studio D. Miriam Watkins wanted to unite the Latin community and share her love of dance with everyone in Tallahassee. In 2013 she opened Studio D. Time your visit just right because Studio D is the only place in Tallahassee with monthly socials, salsa nights on the 2nd Wednesday of the month, and Bachata Fever on the 1st Thursday of the month. You can dance every day at Studio D while you choose between an extensive list of classes, socials, private lessons, events, group classes, or day-long boot camps. Learn salsa, merengue, mambo, and cha-cha in our capital city submerging yourself in the love of music and dance. Don't be nervous! When you step into Studio D you will immediately feel the warmth and energy of the instructors. They will make you feel welcomed and comfortable and get you dancing in no time. No one would ever know you learned to dance in Tallahassee; it will be our little secret.

2525 Apalachee Pkwy., Ste. 8
850-224-0076, studiodtally.com

FEEL THE VIBE
AT BLUE TAVERN

You would never know it is there, but once you do you will always come back. Blue Tavern is a hole-in-the-wall pub with live music nightly, from bluegrass to jazz and even an open mic night. Their welcoming yet calming vibe with unbelievably talented artists makes any night memorable. You can eat, drink coffee, or find a drink that lifts your soul. Located in the heart of Midtown and within walking distance of three of Tallahassee's historic, eclectic, and trendy neighborhoods—Frenchtown, Levy Park, and Lafayette Park—Blue Tavern is a place to connect, be surrounded by good company, and enjoy a night filled with art, music, and absolutely no TV. Their staff is amazing and they love to sing along with the artists as they pour drinks.

1206 N Monroe St.
850-815-8566, bluetaverntallahassee.com

GATHER AROUND
AT THE HUB AT FEATHER OAKS

Indoor and outdoor event spaces at a historic farm were re-imagined and repurposed for everyone to enjoy at the Hub at Feather Oaks. Located only 15 minutes from downtown Tallahassee, and steps away from the Miccosukee Greenway, the Hub is the new weekend place to gather, make friends, and enjoy live music. Hubs and Hops bike shop from Thomasville, Georgia, has opened its doors on-site for bike rentals, sales, and tune-ups. The Hub at Feather Oaks is the only place in Tallahassee where you can park, rent, or bring your bike, hop on the trails, and enjoy craft beer, food trucks, live music, and games afterwards. Suitable for the entire family, the Hub provides a refreshing, relaxed, and fun atmosphere where you can hang out all day. A truly unique and beautiful space surrounded by nature, a vineyard, and a stage under the perfect tree, the Hub is the place to be.

6500 Miccosukee Rd.
850-559-0424, thehubatfeatheroaks.com

41

SKIP BROADWAY AND WATCH A SHOW
AT FSU, FAMU, OR THEATRE TCC!

Arts, culture, and history flourish in Tallahassee, but there is nothing like visiting a true college town and watching the soon-to-be world-renowned artists. Before you see them perform on a Broadway or Chicago stage or in a Hollywood movie, you will have the opportunity to see them in Tallahassee. The School of Theatre at Florida State University has its season from October through April and offers a wide variety of plays and musicals in any one of their theaters—Fallon, Lab, or Conradi Studio Theatre. The FAMU Essential Theatre at Florida A&M University provides an emphasis on African American culture from classical to contemporary plays, and Theatre TCC! at Tallahassee Community College offers a full-season program at the Turner Auditorium where students are allowed to explore their talents and engage their imaginations. Nothing beats a live performance, and a night out in one of these theaters is sure to make a positive lasting impression.

FSU Fine Arts School of Theatre
540 W Call St.
850-644-6500, tickets.theatre.fsu.edu/online

The FAMU Essential Theatre
515 Orr Dr.
850-561-2425, cssah.famu.edu/departments-and-centers/essential-theatre/index.php

Theatre TCC!
444 Appleyard Dr.
850-201-6074, tcc.fl.edu/student-life/arts-and-culture/theatre-tcc

SEE IT ALL
AT THE HOUSE OF MUSIC

The Tallahassee music scene is alive, vibrant, and happening daily at the House of Music. In 2014, the Junction at Monroe opened to provide a welcoming music scene to Tallahassee, and in March 2022 it came back as the House of Music. The best nights out are usually spent in eclectic, unique places like the House of Music, which is filled with community history, great music, and good food. This is a place where you come to simply have a good time. It is a 1930s warehouse with 80-year-old wood flooring and exposed brick walls filled with art, vintage items, and collectibles for sale. Everything from bingo, karaoke, comedy, and even dinner nights are held at the House of Music. Grab a seat, order a drink, get some food, and enjoy the only place in Tallahassee where multigenre live music is played almost every night.

2011 S Monroe St.
850-629-9526, houseofmusictally.com

HAVE A GOOD TIME
AT DISTRICT 850 AND HANGAR 38

Take a break from the outdoors and experience indoor fun and entertainment all under one roof. It's time to create memories with your friends, partner, kids, or even coworkers. On-site restaurants, a full bar, and plenty of challenging and fun experiences make District 850 and Hangar 38 places where there is something for everyone. Enjoy a night out playing pool or axe throwing. The possibilities are endless: bowling, arcade games, escape rooms, laser tag, ropes course, and VIP rooms for kids, adults, and even clubs. Become a pinball master while listening to music and watching sports. In these two enormous venues, parents and kids can enjoy themselves under a combined total of 57,000 square feet. Hangar 38 is conveniently located in the Bannerman Crossings, and District 850 is in the Canopy subdivision off Walaunee Boulevard.

District 850
2662 Fleischmann Way
850-513-2123, district850.com

Hangar 38
6668 Thomasville Rd.
850-999-2606, thehangar38.com

TIP

Run, hike, or bike the Miccosukee Greenway off Fleischmann Road and head over to District 850 to fill up and have some fun.

LAUGH, DANCE, OR DRINK ALL NIGHT AT FIRE BETTY'S ARCADE BAR AND FINNEGAN'S WAKE IRISH PUB

Tallahassee has an infinite number of shows every night, but one thing is certain—most Tuesdays it is comedy night at Fire Betty's Arcade Bar. Reduce your mental load, release some endorphins, and even work on your abs as you enjoy the benefits of laughter with some of the best local and regional comedians. Want to work on your cardio? Dance parties take place every Friday and Saturday as you Dance with a DJ. Located in the heart of Midtown, Fire Betty's Arcade is the place to have some fun with amazing live music, karaoke night for you to sing your heart out, great drinks, themed nights, and pinball machines, all of which make this place a go-to hangout.

More in the mood for a low-key night out? Head a few doors down to Finnegan's Wake Irish Pub, the place to hang out with your friends while playing pool, foosball, or air hockey. It is the only Irish pub in the city and a great place to enjoy a BOGO (buy one, get one free) happy hour. Whether it is a trivia, bingo, or open mic night, be ready for a night of fun and plenty of Irish-inspired food. You are sure to have a good time, especially if you hit both on the same night!

Fire Betty's Arcade Bar
1122 Thomasville Rd., Ste. 1
850-329-8113, facebook.com/firebettys

Finnegan's Wake Irish Pub
1122 Thomasville Rd., #2
850-329-8113, finnspub.com

BARHOP IN MIDTOWN

Brass Tap
1321 Thomasville Rd.
850-320-6300, brasstapbeerbar.com/midtowntallahassee

Over Under
1240 Thomasville Rd.
850-597-7552, overunderbar.com

Liberty Bar
1307 N Monroe St.
850-354-8277, libertytlh.com

Hummingbird Wine Bar
1216-4 N Monroe St.
850-296-2766, hummingbird.wine

The Leon Pub
215 E 6th Ave.
850-425-4639, leonpub.com

FUMA Cigar Social
1307 N Monroe St.
850-765-5756, fumacigarsocial.com

FSU *Unconquered* statue

SPORTS AND RECREATION

45

FEAR THE SPEAR
AT FLORIDA STATE UNIVERSITY

You have not seen Tallahassee energy until you find yourself surrounded by 80,000 fans chanting the FSU War Chant at Doak Campbell Stadium! Florida State University football season in Tallahassee is intense. Walk down the streets and experience life in a college town. Take it all in as everyone tailgates with music, plenty of food, drinks, family, and friends in the intramural fields, in College Town, or down Jackson Bluff Road. One thing is certain, everyone bleeds garnet and gold on game days! Florida State University athletics teams are the best in the nation and provide amazing live entertainment. Be ready to enjoy a fun-filled season with an incredible roster of men's and women's sports in basketball, baseball at the Dick Howser Stadium, softball, swimming and diving, tennis, soccer, volleyball, cross country, track, golf, and more. FSU has it all!

600 W College Ave.
850-644-2525, fsu.edu, seminoles.com

TIP

Get a ride from Capital City Pedicabs, and don't leave Tallahassee without spotting one of FSU's traditions, the Garnet and Gold Guys!

46

TRY A TRI
AT RED HILLS TRIATHLON

For over 20 years, Tallahassee has been home to a sanctioned triathlon race that takes place inside one of Florida's most beautiful green spaces, Alfred B. Maclay Gardens State Park. The swimming portion of the Red Hills triathlon takes place in the waters of Lake Hall with temperatures in the low 70s, followed by a challenging and hilly cycling course up one of Tallahassee's most scenic canopy roads, and ending with a section that allows runners to witness Tallahassee's natural spring beauty on paved and off-road trails inside the park. Finish surrounded by your fans in the Gulf Winds Triathlon community and enjoy food, music, and awards at the picnic pavilion. It's a one-third-mile swim, a 19.3-mile bike, a 5K run, and a super sprint is also available.

It's time to TRI in the capital city!

3540 Thomasville Rd.
redhillstri.com

47

FISH
AT THE ST. MARKS RIVER

Only 10 miles from Tallahassee, you can learn what is meant by the term "Forgotten Coast" at St. Marks River. If you are a fisherman, this is where dreams come true, as redfish, flounder, and trophy speck trout are always present. The St. Marks will eventually enter the waters of the Wakulla River leading out to Apalachee Bay, and a well-marked channel will lead you safely on to the Gulf of Mexico. It is a beautiful, scenic, and historic ride as you are mesmerized by the beauty of the waters and pockets of stillness alongside the St. Marks Natural Wildlife Refuge, where birds, eagles, turtles, manatees, and gators all cohabitate in and around the waters. St. Marks is a great option for enjoying the coastline, and a view of St. Marks's historic working lighthouse is always available to guide your way. Get wet, enjoy the sandbars, and mellow out on the 200-acre rock garden off the coast.

148 Old Fort Rd., St. Marks

TIP

If you go down to the St. Marks River, rent a pontoon boat, kayak, or paddleboat at Shields Marina (shieldsmarina.com) and enjoy a full or half day out on the waters. Boating is a perfect way to spend the day with family, go fishing, or simply discover the area. Watch the sunset at Riverside Cafe right on the river (riversidebay.com) and don't leave without grabbing a bite at the Cooter Stew Cafe.

SNAP FOR INSTAGRAM
AT ST. MARKS NATIONAL WILDLIFE REFUGE

Don't be one of those visitors that come to Tallahassee and don't make their way to the St. Marks National Wildlife Refuge. Established in 1931 as a winter habitat for migratory birds that encompasses over 83,000 acres along three different counties and 43 miles of Florida's Gulf coastline, St. Marks NWR is a sanctuary the public can enjoy. A diverse array of over 400 species of wildlife includes bobcats, eagles, deer, birds, monarch butterflies, and alligators that can often be glimpsed on your own, but don't miss out on the guided tours behind the gate. This wildlife refuge is also home to the historic working St. Marks Lighthouse at the end of the road and has an extensive trail system perfect for hiking or biking. Many fishermen try their luck on the wetlands along the road, while others kayak along the coast. Arrive early to catch a magical sunrise and/or stay long enough to catch a stunning sunset over Apalachee Bay with your camera, so you will never forget your day at St. Marks.

1255 Lighthouse Rd., St. Marks
850-925-6121, fws.gov/refuge/st-marks

TIP

The grand butterfly migration takes place in October.

FIND THE BIG BLUE
AT WACISSA RIVER

Submerge yourself in the crystal-clear waters of one of the state's most beautiful freshwater tracts, the Wacissa River. Fed by more than 20 springs and stretching 10 miles to end at the primitive Good Pasture Campground, the Wacissa River is beloved by locals for its swimming, snorkeling, canoeing, kayaking, fishing, and even duck hunting possibilities. Some days it feels like a never-ending party as music and people can be heard almost two miles down as you approach the entry to the river's most popular swimming hole, Blue Spring. Adventure seekers go on shore to jump off ropes that dangle from various overhanging trees. Explorers like to dive or swim in the mouth of the hole. Others just want to take it all in. However, most days it is fairly quiet, and the serene waters provide the solitude, peace, and tranquility that allow you to reflect surrounded by the wonders of nature. Be aware and respectful of the wildlife all around you—turtles, birds, river otters, and of course, alligators.

One of North Florida's best-kept secrets!

290 Wacissa Springs Rd., Monticello

TIP

Rent a kayak or canoe at wacissarivercanoerentals.com.

DO IT ALL
AT LAFAYETTE HERITAGE TRAIL

It is impossible not to notice the greenery that surrounds the capital city. With dozens of trails nearby, you will be sure to find one you like, one that will challenge you and another one that will keep you coming back to Tallahassee. Most likely, the one that entices you will be Lafayette Heritage Trail, one of the most beautiful trails in Tallahassee, where you can hike, mountain bike, fish, paddle, kayak, and even bird-watch. The wildlife is omnipresent beneath the beautiful oak trees. Walk on the train tracks, experience both worlds on the man-made land bridge, feel the energy of the train as you watch from the bridge above, and get lost in the trails surrounding the beautiful Piney Z Lake (Lake Lafayette). This is Tallahassee's version of an enchanted forest where everything is real. Ride the challenging single-track Cadillac and Magnolia trails and don't leave without admiring the solo cypress tree that can be seen from the bridge.

There is no better place to watch the sunset than on the land bridge!

49000 Heritage Park Blvd. or 2500 Pedrick Rd.
850-891-3866, talgov.com/parks/parks-trail-lafayette

TIP

There is a special week in December when white pelicans can be seen from the trail.

51

EXPERIENCE HISTORY AND NATURE

AT TALLAHASSEE-ST. MARKS HISTORIC STATE RAILROAD TRAIL

Tallahassee-St. Marks Historic State Railroad Trail was the first rail trail in Florida's system of greenways to be paved. It had been part of the longest operating railroad corridor, carrying cotton from the plantations to the coast, but now it serves as a network of enjoyable trails covered by long-leaf pine.

The trail extends 16 miles from its main trailhead to end at the small fishing community of St. Marks—right on the water and only steps away from San Marcos de Apalache Historic State Park. Suitable for walking, hiking, running, skating, cycling, mountain biking, and even horseback riding in some areas, the Tallahassee-St. Marks Historic State Railroad Trail is accessible to anyone. From it, you can hike a portion of the Florida National Scenic Trail, mountain bike the Munson trails inside the Apalachicola National Forest, or take a detour around mile nine and head over to Edward Ball Wakulla Springs State Park. Whatever you do, enjoy the journey!

4478 Woodville Hwy.
850-245-2081, floridastateparks.org/parks-and-trails/
tallahassee-st-marks-historic-railroad-state-trail

Want to ride 32 miles? Bring water, snacks, and money as you ride to St. Marks. Enjoy lunch by the river, and on your way back detour by Edward Ball Wakulla Springs State Park and take a dip in the cold waters to rejuvenate as you make your way back to Tallahassee.

52

EXPLORE
FLORIDA STATE PARKS

Tallahassee is all about enjoying the outdoors. Unlike any other region in Florida, Tallahassee offers a combination of beautiful rolling hills and endless miles of canopy roads. The Florida Parks Service has 175 parks—one of which is the largest in the country—and Tallahassee is home to several of them. Our Tallahassee parks are:

- St. Marks River Preserve State Park
- Tallahassee-St.Marks Historic Railroad State Trail
- Natural Bridge Battlefield Historic State Park
- Lake Jackson Mounds Archeological State Park
- Alfred B. Maclay Gardens State Park
- Lake Talquin State Park
- Letchworth-Love Mounds Archaeological State Park

The others are just a short drive outside the city limits:

- Edward Ball Wakulla Springs State Park
- San Marcos de Apalache Historic State Park
- Bald Point State Park
- Econfina River State Park
- Torreya State Park
- Florida Caverns State Park
- Three Rivers State Park
- Forest Capital Museum State Park
- Dr. Julian G. Bruce St. George Island State Park
- Ochlockkonee River State Park

floridastateparks.org

53

STROLL THROUGH
CASCADES PARK

What was a gathering spot for hunters and travelers in the 19th century with winding trails filled with history now serves as one of Tallahassee's best urban parks. Step onto the initial point from which all land surveying began in the state of Florida in 1824, the Meridian Marker. Beginning as Tallahassee's first public water system in the 1890s, segueing to a power and light plant in 1921, and repurposed as Centennial Field in 1925 where FSU's first three football seasons were played, Cascades Park has turned into a dynamic destination that connects the soul of this community. The park features 2.3 miles of trails; a commemoration site that pays tribute to the once-thriving African American community of Smokey Hollow; a public lynching historical marker; a Korean War Memorial; play areas for kids where the water, lights, and music of the Imagination Fountain capture any child's heart; a restaurant; a fountain; the Adderley Capital City Amphitheater; and a gateway to FAMU Way!

It also has the charm of the waterfall where Tallahassee began!

TIP

Take an adventure from this urban park out to the coast. Follow the trails of Cascades Park onto FAMU Way and head on over to Tallahassee-St. Marks Historic Railroad State Trail. When you return, enjoy any of our local favorite hangouts—the Railroad Square Art District, Proof Brewing, Amicus Brewing, the Edison restaurant, or Charlie Park.

ENJOY A BEAUTIFUL MASTERPIECE

AT ALFRED B. MACLAY GARDENS STATE PARK

Over 1,000 acres of botanical wonders, history, multiuse trails, and water activities await at Alfred B. Maclay Gardens State Park. Fascinated by the size of the oak and pine trees and the beauty of the dogwoods and hollies, Mr. Maclay purchased the home in the 1920s to serve as his winter getaway and to create a beautiful garden, which was later donated by Mrs. Maclay to the state of Florida in 1953 for the people to enjoy. Today, the Alfred B. Maclay Gardens State Park includes some of America's most beautiful gardens and has its own US postal stamp. Moss-covered trees protect the brick walkway leading into sections with hundreds of flowers, a secret garden, a reflection pool, and a majestic view of Lake Hall from the front steps of the house. Swim, fish, run, hike, bike, paddle, kayak, or throw a blanket down and rest by the abundant beauty of camellias and azaleas.

3540 Thomasville Rd.
850-487-4556, floridastateparks.org/MaclayGardens

TIP

The peak season to enjoy the blooms is January through April with the best viewing in mid- to late March. These are also the only times when you can tour the Maclay house.

55

SEE OLD FLORIDA

AT EDWARD BALL WAKULLA SPRINGS STATE PARK

Get on that two-story platform and dive into one of the world's largest freshwater springs at Edward Ball Wakulla Springs State Park. With water temperatures in the 70s, Wakulla Springs is simply the best place to be during a hot Florida summer. Kayak or do a jungle cruise tour down the mysterious waters where you are guaranteed to see birds, alligators, turtles, fish, and the beloved, gentle, and enormous manatee. Swim or snorkel in waters once canoed by early Native Americans and experience primitive life, the ancient cypress swamps, trails inside the forest, and even a real North Florida castle. Built in 1937 by Edward Ball, the Lodge at Wakulla Springs is one of the few castles in the state where you can stay overnight. Wake up to the sapphire waters of Wakulla Springs, enjoy the nine miles of trails, take a tour into Florida's elegant past, and witness the largest marble soda fountain ever built!

465 Wakulla Park Dr., Wakulla Springs
850-561-7276, floridastateparks.org/WakullaSprings

TIP

Wakulla Springs is perfect for a day out with the kids or to ride your bike on the St. Marks Trail out to the coast. Visit our secret Cherokee Sinks less than two miles down the road, then spend the night at the Wakulla Lodge.

56

BIKE, HIKE, AND HORSE-BACK RIDE THE TRAILS
AT J. R. ALFORD GREENWAY

Immerse yourself in over 800 acres of pasture and woodlands as you stroll or cycle down the perfectly crushed oyster shell paths and secluded canopy trails of the J. R. Alford Greenway. Start your adventure in one of Tallahassee's most popular parks, and don't be surprised when your jaw drops as you look out into the wide-open greenway at the end of the road. Enter the tree-lined path and set out to experience the perfect place to lose yourself and not be worried about time. Almost 20 miles of hidden, yet well-marked, trails loop you around rideable open fields filled with wildflowers. Birds are ever present and the sound of duck hunting, a distant train, and overhead planes can often be heard as you enjoy a newfound ride. While black bears do inhabit the area, you are more likely to see deer and the occasional snake along your path. Never the same twice!

2500 Pedrick Rd.
850-606-1470, cms.leoncountyfl.gov/home/departments/office-of-resource-stewardship/parks-and-recreation

Bike Tallahassee
biketallahassee.com

Capital City Cyclists
cccyclists.org

Tallahassee Mountain Biking Association
tmba.bike

Gulf Winds Triathletes
gulfwindstri.com

EXPLORE THESE TRAILS

To the right of the J. R. Alford Greenway, is the gateway to **Lafayette Heritage Park**.
talgov.com/parks/parks-trail-lafayette

Ready to mountain bike? For twists and turns, ride the Red Bug Trail in **Elinor Klapp-Phipps Park**.
talgov.com/parks/parks-phipps

For speed, ride **Munson Hills in the Apalachicola National Forest**.
fs.usda.gov/main/florida/home

For single-track dives, ride **Tom Brown Park**.
talgov.com/parks/parks-tombrown

For man-made jumps, ride **Cadillac Mountain Bike Trail at Lafayette Heritage Park**.
talgov.com/parks/parks-trail-lafayette

For an easier and more enjoyable ride, try **Miccosukee Greenway**.
cms.leoncountyfl.gov/home/departments/office-of-resource-stewardship/parks-and-recreation/greenways?page23371=1&size23371=50

Tallahassee Leon County Park Finder
tlcgis.leoncountyfl.gov/ParkFinder/index.html?find=miccosukee%20canopy%20road%20greenway

Download the Tally Parks app to get them all.

TIP

Tallahassee is home to a robust gravel-biking, cycling, and mountain-biking community. Reach out to them when you visit for information on group rides, special places to bike, events, and races.

CLIMB THE TREES
AT TALLAHASSEE MUSEUM TREE-TO-TREE ADVENTURE

Explore the ground below from up to 60 feet high on the Tree-to-Tree Adventure at the Tallahassee Museum. Glide over 52 acres of animals nestled in their native Florida habitats, beautiful cypress swamps, incredible flora, historic buildings, and even Jim Gary's 20th Century Dinosaurs exhibition. With up to 47 platforms, visitors can move safely from tree to tree as they test their skills over wobbly bridges, tightropes, crab walks, jungle bridges, and nets. Three different courses will quench your thirst for adventure in the capital city and ensure you have a great time! Enjoy the outdoors in this unique oasis only steps away from Florida State University's campus, and finish with an unbelievably fast and unforgettable glide over Lake Bradford.

You are here to create some long-lasting memories, so get up on that tree trail and let the adventure begin!

3945 Museum Dr.
850-575-8684, tallahasseemuseum.org

RUN

THE TALLAHASSEE MARATHON AND HALF MARATHON

The humble beginnings of the Tallahassee Marathon began on March 8, 1975, with only two participants. Since then, it has drawn thousands of people from all over the world. On February 11, 1984, the half marathon started and was finished by 149 participants. Throughout the years, the start and finish lines have changed. Whether the course has been flat or hilly, the dedication of the volunteers who run this event—organized by the local running group Gulf Winds Track Club—has remained. In 2016, race director Ely Rosario worked with the City of Tallahassee to unveil a permanent finish line unlike any other in the nation for the marathon in downtown Tallahassee right across Duval Plaza. Currently, the race takes runners through beautiful, energetic, and historic sites throughout the city, finishing in College Town.

This race has done so much for so many; it's time for you to participate in it and let it do something for you!

tallahasseemarathon.com

TIP

Tallahassee is home to a very active running community. Make sure to check out the local Gulf Winds Track Club and search for more than 100 races year-round.

gulfwinds.org

59

LET'S CLIMB
AT ALCHEMY CLIMBING

Alchemy Climbing, previously known as Tallahassee Rock Gym, led the way as the first dedicated climbing gym in Florida when it opened its doors close to Florida State University in 1995. In 2021, the gym moved from its 20-year-old location on Railroad Square to Tallahassee's old discount movie theater, Movies 8. Alchemy Climbing has expanded into a diverse community that celebrates climbing as a way to work on reaching its potential, whatever that may be. Instructors at Alchemy suggest that climbers wear comfortable long pants and sleeved shirts to enjoy the sport of indoor climbing in the Red Hills Region. Climb and descend with or without a rope, challenge yourself, have fun, and meet new people—all under one roof! Auto belay, top rope, lead climbing, bouldering, and yoga classes are all offered at Alchemy, but don't worry, no experience is required. You will be guided by their experts. In addition, teams, classes, group events, clinics, and summer camps are available.

2810 Sharer Rd.
850-224-7625, alchemyclimbing.com

REJOICE
AT THE MOON

In 1985, Scott Carswell opened the Moon. Since then, this space has brought an enormous gift of diversity into our community. Over 3,000 events have been hosted in this venue, which serves as North Florida's primary community art center. It was the only venue that changed genres from night to night: from country music to hip-hop, classical to jazz, and even plays and community events, all have found a warm home at the Moon. Kenny Chesney, Jimmy Buffett, 69 Boyz, Red Hot Chili Peppers, T-Pain, DJ Laz, and the Temptations have all set foot on this stage. For Tallahassee natives here during the '90s, two words—"Teen Nights"—evoke flashbacks to a few hours of total freedom in an almost-adult environment dancing hip-hop with friends and lounging in a dark atmosphere. The Moon is not only a premier place to dance, but it is also where everyone has always been welcome!

1105 E Lafayette St.
850-878-6900, moonevents.com

61

DRIVE
TO THE BEACH

Tallahassee is a quick adventures-and-escapes ride away from some of the world's most beautiful beaches located less than 100 miles away. Without high-rises, strip malls, or tourist traps, the "Forgotten Coast" beaches are gorgeous and tranquil with abundant activities such as fishing, swimming, kayaking, star gazing, camping, and cycling.. Don't want to travel too far?

- The St. Marks National Wildlife Refuge is less than 25 miles from Tally with visible wildlife, trails, and a unique stretch of beach.
- Mashes Sands, located in Panacea, Florida, is a secluded beach only 35 miles away overlooking the Ochlockonee River with shallow waters.
- Carrabelle Beach is 55 miles out and truly takes you back in time. Miles of sandy, pristine beach scattered with old-school pavilions that provide comfortable shade hide in a small coastal town that is the perfect place to take the family.
- St. George Island, where every Tally native goes, is home to the Dr. Julian G Bruce St. George Island State Park and ranked as the best beach in America in 2023 by Dr. Beach with breathtaking beaches on a 22-mile barrier island in the Gulf of Mexico is 78 miles away.
- Ninety-eight miles out is Cape San Blas, a beach with a laid-back vibe on a narrow stretch of land.

The drive out is almost as beautiful as your beach destination!

St. Marks National Wildlife Refuge
1255 Lighthouse Rd., St. Marks
850-925-6121, fws.gov/refuge/st-marks

Mashes Sands Beach
801 Mashes Sands Rd., Panacea
850-745-7780, mywakulla.com/departments/parks/mashes_sands.php

Carrabelle Beach
1786–2402 Big Bend Scenic Byway Coastal Trail (US 98), Carrabelle

St. George Island
St. George Island
floridasforgottencoast.com/st-george-island

Cape San Blas
Cape San Blas, Port Saint Joe
visitgulf.com/destinations/cape-san-blas

TEE OFF
AT CAPITAL CITY COUNTRY CLUB AND JAKE GAITHER GOLF CLUB

Tallahassee can deliver affordable, rewarding, and uncongested golf experiences with a great view. Ranked as the 13th-best course in the state of Florida and the best one in Tallahassee by *Golfweek* and *USA Today* in 2021, Capital City Country Club is known as the Dream Course of the Southeast. Located inside the historic Myers Park district and adjacent to Cascades Park, the Capital City Country Club is surrounded by gorgeous moss-draped oaks and offers over 250 feet of elevation change. On the south side of Tallahassee, visit one of the only two courses in the state of Florida where African Americans were allowed to play in our community in the 1950s, Jake Gaither Golf Course. Operated by the City of Tallahassee, the course offers nine holes and rolling hills, and it's an ideal place to bring the kids to learn to play the game.

Capital City Country Club
1601 Golf Terrace Dr.
850-222-0419, capitalcitycc.com

Jake Gaither Golf Course
801 Bragg Dr.
850-891-3942, talgov.com/page/jakegaither

TAKE A SWING AT THESE GOLF COURSES

Southwood
3750 Grove Park Dr.
850-942-4653, southwoodgolf.com

Hilaman Golf Course
2737 N Blair Stone Rd.
850-891-2560, talgov.com/page/hilaman

Seminole Legacy Golf Club
2550 Pottsdamer St.
850-645-4653, seminolelegacygolfclub.com

Golden Eagle Golf and Country Club
3700 Golden Eagle Dr. E
850-893-7700, goldeneaglecc.org

EXPERIENCE AWESOME
AT FSU REZ LAKEFRONT PARK

Located on Lake Bradford and overseeing the natural wonders of the Tallahassee Museum is the FSU Rez Lakefront Park, or "The Rez" as it is locally known. The Rez is located only 4 miles from Florida State University and it offers 73 acres for a complete and awesome day of fun. Grab a lounge chair on the sandy beach by the designated swim area to enjoy the rays, or head out into a water adventure. Kayaks, paddleboards, canoes, and even sailboats can be rented for a minimal fee. Exploring the lake can take you into a beautiful cypress swamp corridor, which borders the Tallahassee Museum and segues into Lake Hiawatha, where it later connects to Lake Cascade if you want more water time. On dry land, you can play sand volleyball, horseshoes, cornhole, spike ball, or disc golf. And if you want to be off the ground, have fun climbing the Rez's 40-foot wall.

3226 Flastacowo Rd.
850-644-6892, campusrec.fsu.edu/outdoors/rez

WATCH THE EAGLES SOAR

AT TALLAHASSEE COMMUNITY COLLEGE MEN'S BASKETBALL

Walk in, take a seat, and feel the energy at the Tallahassee Community College Lifetime Sports Complex. Located in the center of the TCC campus, the complex offers three indoor multisport courts and is home to Tallahassee Community College men's and women's basketball teams. The TCC men's basketball team was led by coach Rick Cabrera from 2021 to 2023. In 2023 Corey Hendren was named the sixth head coach in the 31-year history of the program. The talent, hard work, and enthusiasm of the athletes is the hallmark of every game and even ESPN+ pays a visit from time to time to see these athletes play. In the smaller and more inviting venue, fans feel as if every seat is courtside, so you will have an excellent view of the games from any seat in the house. Tallahassee Community College is a member of the National Junior College Athletic Association (NJCAA). They play in the Panhandle Conference, which is arguably the SEC of the NJCAA.

Wear your blue and gold and come watch the Eagles fly!

444 Appleyard Dr.
tcceagles.com/landing/index

65

SKATE AGAIN
AT SKATEABLE ART PARK AT FAMU WAY

It is time to test your skills and tackle the 225-foot-long snake run that is the centerpiece of Tallahassee's Skateable Art Park on FAMU Way. The park opened in 2021 in the heart of Tallahassee, right under one of our seven magical hills off FAMU and next to the city's Railroad Square art district. The rattler speed bump sculpture pays tribute to Florida A&M University, whose mascot is a rattlesnake. The park is filled with art from local artists, a graffiti wall, plenty of curves and changes in elevations, rails, and walls to improve your Rollerblade, cycling, or skateboarding skills. It has brought together a community of people who want to learn to use their skateboards, skates, BMX bikes, and even scooters along with those who want to get back into it. On any given day, you will see a range of demographics, from young and college-age kids to older adults who want to have a good time either by participating in the sports or by sitting down and enjoying watching people do what they love.

810 Famu Way

TEST OUT THESE SKATE PARKS

The Secret Skatepark
1039 S Duval St.

Mike Blankenship Skate Park
2909 Jackson Bluff Rd.

Skate World
2563 Capital Cir. NE
850-385-7465, skateworld1.com

TOUR THE SKIES
WITH TALLAHASSEE HELICOPTERS

Like many great cities, Tallahassee is a well-kept secret that hides its beauty, but Tallahassee Helicopters helps you see it all. The company offers flight lessons and pilot training, yet it is the scenic tours and adventure flights that captivate visitors to the capital city. Unlike other tourist attractions, Tallahassee Helicopters can customize any flight as long as it is FAA-compliant, of course. If you are not sure what you want to see, select one of their 10 different tours ranging from city limits out to the coast. It is a unique, relaxed, and smooth way to see the beauty and attractions of Tallahassee.

3240 Capital Cir. SW, Ste. 1
850-841-1111, tallahassee-helicopters.com

TIP

As you fly over Tallahassee, you will marvel at the vast amount of tree coverage all over our city. Hot air balloon rides are another way to tour the Tallahassee skies.

tropicalbreesesballooningadventures.com

67

KAYAK OR PADDLEBOARD
THE WAKULLA RIVER

Looking for an easy, relaxing, and scenic way to explore the waters of the Wakulla River? Kayak or paddle a canoe or SUP down a three- or six-mile route on the cool and often clear waters of the river. Launch at the public boat ramp on Highway 98 and let the current carry you along. The river is lined with trees on both sides, and houses in various conditions can be seen tucked back in along the way. The docks lining the banks are private, so do not stop to use them without permission. As you enjoy the waters, keep an eye out for the several different bird species that inhabit the trees and brush along your route, along with the many turtles sunning on branches, rocks, and trunks halfway submerged in the waters. If you are lucky, on warmer days you might catch a glimpse of a gentle, slow-moving manatee or the occasional gator along the bank. The trip will not always be tranquil. Sometimes, the river is filled with boaters and tubers playing music and having a great time, which adds to the sense of adventure.

Take Hwy. 363 (Woodville Hwy.) 18 miles south to State Rd. 98 (Coastal Hwy.)
Turn right and drive west two miles

TIP

You can rent a kayak or get a guided tour of the Wakulla River at TNT Hideaway. Make your reservations in advance.

6527 Coastal Hwy., Crawfordville
850-925-6412, tnthideaway.com

ENJOY
THE CITY OF TALLAHASSEE PARKS

By 2024, the City of Tallahassee will have 100 parks available for everyone to enjoy. In a city surrounded by nature, the love of the outdoors lives and thrives in this community. Visitors can participate in all the activities available in each park as if they were residents of this community. No special passes will be required. Whatever outdoor activities you like to indulge in, they are available to you in the capital city. There are pools for lap swimming or shallow activity pools for the kids. If you like active sports, there are opportunities to volley with family members or friends on our tennis, racquetball, or pickleball courts. Play the number one disc golf course in Florida, spike your opponent's serve on our sand volleyball courts, or join a pickup game on public park basketball courts. Barbecue in designated picnic areas and launch your boat, kayak, or canoe from park boat ramps. Hike, bike, horseback ride, and bird watch on the many and varied greenway trails. Get excited, get moving, and fall in love with our outdoors.

City of Tallahassee Parks and Rec
1201 Myers Park Dr.
850-891-3866, talgov.com/parks/parks, talgov.com/gis/parks_trails

TIP

Download the City of Tallahassee parks app, Tally Parks, for an interactive experience.

TRY OUT THESE ACTIVE CLUBS

Gulf Winds Track Club
gulfwinds.org

Gulf Winds Triathletes
gulfwindstri.com

Tallahassee Mountain Biking Association
tmba.bike

Tallahassee Archery Club
bigbendarchery.com

Shell Point Sailboard Club
spsc20knotsnob.com

Tallahassee Rowing Club
tallahasseerowing.weebly.com

Capital City Cyclists
cccyclists.org

Tallahassee Disc Golf Association
discgolftally.org

Florida Trail Association
apalachee.floridatrail.org

Tallahassee Roller Girls
tallahasseerollerderby.com

Tallahassee Tennis Association
ttatennis.org

Scuba Dive Club
facebook.com/wakulladivingcenter

Tallahassee Pickleball Association
tallahasseepickleball.com

Tallahassee Tarpon Underwater Rugby Club
facebook.com/people/tallahassee-tarpon-underwater-rugby-club-tturc/100063487535059

Seminole Scuba Club
campusrec.fsu.edu/sports/clubs/scuba-club

GOODWOOD
(2 MILES EAST ON LAFAYETTE GRANT)
ANTE-BELLUM MANSION CONSTRUCTED OF BRICK SHIPPED FROM NEW YORK TO PORT OF ST. MARKS. COMPLETED IN 1843. FINE FAN LIGHTS AND PLEASING WINDOW PLACEMENTS. CIRCULAR STAIRWAY. RARE OLD FURNISHINGS.
DONATED BY THE CITY OF TALLAHASSEE.

CULTURE AND HISTORY

69

SAVOR HISTORY
AT BRADLEY'S COUNTRY STORE

Almost 100 years of history and tradition stand in one humble, small, yet unforgettable place, Bradley's Country Store. Step back in time in this four generation family owned business best known for its famous Bradley sausages. Built in 1927, the building is listed in the National Register of Historic places. Enjoy the 12 mile ride from the center of town, park under the grandiose oak trees covered in Spanish moss and enter a world that has stood the test of time. A delicious smell of homemade sausage will welcome you while the uniqueness of the place will truly enchant you. Seasonings, raw and cooked meats, jellies, candy, drinks, honey, grits, local history books, and plenty of souvenirs are only a few of the items you will find at Bradley's Country Store. You simply can not miss Bradley's Fun Day on the Saturday before Thanksgiving. A tradition that started in 1970 for the community to enjoy a day filled with hundreds of vendors, live music, cane grinding, syrup making, and an abundance of food.

10655 Centerville Rd.
850-893-4742, bradleyscountrystore.com

Around the corner from Bradley’s Country Store is Old Centerville Road, a beautiful 6 mile unpaved road that ends in Georgia, perfect for running or biking under a shaded canopy road. Many runners and cyclists park at the store to enjoy the surrounding roads.

STRIKE, STRIKE, AND STRIKE AGAIN AT FAMU HOMECOMING

Built on the highest of seven hills in 1887, Florida's only historically Black university (HBCU), Florida Agricultural and Mechanical University, known as FAMU, sits tall over the city of Tallahassee. Welcome to the Hill and enjoy FAMU homecoming, a gateway for connecting the entire community. FAMU is a place where multigenerational relationships are established, lifelong friends reunite, and students and people from all over flock to witness, celebrate, and feel the tight bond of the African American community. FAMU homecoming is a weeklong celebration starting with the coronation of Mr. and Miss FAMU. It continues with an impressive step show from the Divine 9, and a comedy show leads to the culmination of all-day Saturday festivities. Starting with the pregame parade, homecoming reaches a crescendo with the football game at Bragg Memorial Stadium and the Marching 100 halftime show. Saturday night winds down with a hip-hop concert. On Sunday, a gospel concert closes the festivities. Experience the traditions and embrace the culture at FAMU. Don't miss the Rattler Show!

1601 S Martin Luther King Jr. Blvd.
850-599-3000, famu.edu

71

ENJOY HISTORY IN NATURE
AT THE TALLAHASSEE MUSEUM

Wear comfortable clothes to step back in time and enjoy the natural beauty distinct to this area at the Tallahassee Museum. Still known to many locals by its original name—the Tallahassee Junior Museum—it was renamed in 1992. The museum was created in 1957 to offer an expanding educational experience to children in science, art, history, and world culture. Today it offers the region an exclusive opportunity to experience what life was like in the South, animal exhibits in their natural habitats, changing exhibits showcasing the region's culture, and a tree-to-tree climbing adventure. History is present on the grounds with the first regularly organized Black church in Florida, Bethlehem Missionary Baptist Church; the Concord School House, built in the late 1870s for the children of former slaves; a glimpse of the life of a train conductor inside the Seaboard Airline Caboose; and the Bellevue Plantation—former home of a princess.

Walk through history on curated grounds surrounded by a chain of lakes and magnificent cypress corridors.

3945 Museum Rd.
850-575-8684, tallahasseemuseum.org

72

WALK DOWN THE MIDDLE
AT OLD CITY CEMETERY

Old City Cemetery is the oldest cemetery in Tallahassee, currently located on the edge of the Park Avenue Chain of Parks and bordering Florida State University. A thoroughly segregated cemetery, it was established in 1829, outside city boundaries where the Whites were laid to rest on the east side and the African Americans on the west. Visitors can walk through the resting place of many of the men who contributed to the development of Florida and Tallahassee, including John Riley, the principal of Lincoln High School; Thomas Brown, a Florida governor; and the Proctors, three generations of Black men who changed history. Casualties of the Civil War Battle of Natural Bridge are also buried here. Union casualties (Black or White) were buried with the Blacks and Confederates with the Whites. Walk down the six-foot-wide path that marks the separation line between Blacks and Whites buried here.

400 W Park Ave.
850-891-8712, talgov.com/realestate/res-coc-oldcity

TIP

Download a walking tour of the city, which includes the cemetery.

visittallahassee.com/heritagetrails_downtown
visitflorida.com/travel-ideas, articles/walking-tour-tallahassee-florida

GET HOOKED
AT THE NATIONAL HIGH MAGNETIC FIELD LABORATORY

An annual spring open house and monthly public tours held on the third Wednesday of each month welcome visitors to a fascinating, ever-changing, and record-breaking world at the National High Magnetic Field Laboratory. Locally known as the MagLab, this famous center is headquartered at FSU and was called the "mecca for scientists and engineers" by Vice President Al Gore. The history of this world-class research center began in 1989 when Jack Crow of FSU, Don Parking of Los Alamos National Laboratory, and Neil Sullivan of UF submitted a proposal to the National Science Foundation to work on the world's most powerful magnets. In 1990, permission to create the National High Magnetic Field Laboratory was awarded to them, making it the only facility of its kind in the US. World records have been broken in resistive, hybrid, and pulsed magnetic fields throughout the years. Researchers, students, and visitors come from all over the world to start, renew, or continue their love for science.

1800 E Paul Dirac Dr.
850-644-0311, nationalmaglab.org

TAKE A WALKING TOUR
OF FLORIDA STATE UNIVERSITY

As you walk through the campus of Florida State University, its historic legacy can be felt with every step. Dating back to 1853, Florida State University is one of the oldest and largest of the 12 institutions of higher learning in the State University System of Florida, with one of the most beautiful campuses in the US. FSU is one of the top 25 universities in the nation, located on grounds with stunning architecture, exquisite gardens, commemorative and historical statues, sculptures, and landmarks. Tour FSU's top-five treasured landmarks and share the students, staff, and faculty's enormous sense of pride as you walk through its campus: Westcott Fountain and Plaza in front of Ruby Diamond Auditorium, a go-to photo stop; Dodd Hall, highlighting its Gothic architecture (inside is the Heritage Museum and an impressive stained glass window that took over a decade to build); *The Integration Statue*, which sits at the end of Woodward Plaza; Legacy Fountain, in Landis Green in front of Strozier Library; and the *Unconquered* statue in front of Doak S. Campbell Stadium.

It is an unforgettable campus!

600 W College Ave.
850-644-2525, fsu.edu, legacywalk.fsu.edu

EXPLORE COLLECTIONS
AT TALLAHASSEE'S ART GALLERIES

Tally gives artists the latitude to experiment and discover, while providing a safe space to grow and develop into a professional artist. Our city nurtures a unique, creative, and vibrant community of artists of all ages and walks of life who fill our galleries with their exceptional work. Three galleries in Tallahassee offer distinct views through the eyes of the artist. If you are looking for boldness and vivid colors, Venvi Gallery offers energetic contemporary art and the unique work of carefully selected artists. If you are not quite sure what you are looking for, step into 4,000 square feet of gallery space with work from more than 50 local, regional, and international artists at Signature Art Gallery. Everything from ethnic work and landscapes to photography and carved-wood sculptures can be found at this gallery. The spacious 621 Gallery offers a diverse community of artists without entry barriers.

The arts live in Tallahassee! Come see them!

Venvi Gallery
2901 E Park Ave., Ste. 2800
850-322-0965
venviartgallery.com

Signature Art Gallery
2782 Capital Cir. NE
850-297-2422
signatureartgallery.com

621 Gallery
650-3 Railroad Sq.
850-222-6210
621gallery.org

LIVE THROUGH HISTORY
AT MISSION SAN LUIS

Visit the past in the beautiful gardens and magnificent structures re-creating the Apalachee Indian and Spanish communities that occupied the area 300 years ago at Mission San Luis. Enter the remnants of what was once a thriving community and tour one of the largest Native American structures ever built in the Southeast, the Council House. Step into the Franciscan Church, the Hispanic Village, and the Friary Complex, and don't leave without seeing the Castillo de San Luis.

The most memorable part of the experience will be the employees and volunteer historians available throughout the grounds. You cannot miss them; they are dressed as San Luis Mission community members in period costumes according to what their duties would have been. They will provide you with a full history lesson at each stop. Don't forget to ask about the dangerous Apalachee ball game, how the choir boys learned their notes, and the political divide that led to the destruction of Mission San Luis.

2100 W Tennessee St.
850-245-6406, missionsanluis.org

SEE THE SHAPING OF THE WORLD
AT THE GROVE MUSEUM

A beautiful structure built by child-slave labor represents 200 years of the history of Tallahassee, the state of Florida, and the United States.

In 1840, Richard Keith Call completed an antebellum plantation house which was eventually known as the Grove. Several generations of the Call and Collins families lived and were buried in the cemetery on the grounds. The property started with over 600 acres, yet throughout the years, financial hardship and business opportunities led to the sale of all but the 10.5 acres that currently sit adjacent to the Governor's Mansion.

In 1942, LeRoy Collins and Mary Call Collins purchased the property, renovated it, and added patios and a two-story Florida room addition. The walls of the Grove Museum witnessed Governor LeRoy Collins's shift from southern man who once stood for segregation to politician with a pro-civil-rights agenda. In 1972, the Grove was listed on the National Register of Historic Places and was sold to the state of Florida in 1985. Today you can learn the history, walk through beautiful gardens, and imagine the historical shifts these walls have seen.

902 N Monroe St.
850-245-6100, thegrovemuseum.com

78

MEET AN ENTREPRENEUR
AT THE JOHN G. RILEY CENTER AND MUSEUM FOR AFRICAN AMERICAN HISTORY AND CULTURE

Born a slave in 1857, John G. Riley was a millionaire by the time of his death in 1954. He built his home at the edge of Smokey Hollow, a once vibrant middle-class African American community in Tallahassee. Currently located at the bottom of a hill in downtown Tallahassee, the John G. Riley Museum tells the remarkable story of a man who was an educator for 49 years, an owner of seven plots of land, and an integral part of the lively history of the African American community in Tallahassee. This beautiful two-story wooden-frame home was built in 1890 and reflected the ability of one man to succeed against all odds.

Walk through John G. Riley's home and get a glimpse of his life, habitat, and livelihood. Learn about the Reconstruction era through workshops, exhibits, and tours provided on-site.

419 E Jefferson St.
850-891-3560, rileymuseum.org

TIP

The Riley Museum is part of a larger walking tour of Tally.

visittallahassee.com/heritagetrails_downtown
visitflorida.com/travel-ideas/articles/walking-tour-tallahassee-florida

PROTECT HISTORY
AT GOODWOOD MUSEUM AND GARDENS

In the heart of Tallahassee, you will find 20 acres remaining of the original 2,400 owned by the Croom family, who came from North Carolina in 1834. Here 60 enslaved African Americans built the main home, grew cotton and corn crops, cleared the land, and performed other daily tasks on the plantation known as Goodwood. The Goodwood Museum and Gardens preserves the historic reality and describes the impact African Americans had on the history of Florida within the four remaining buildings the slaves built at Goodwood.

Today, the Goodwood Museum and Gardens is not only home to historical artifacts but is also available for community and private events. Located in central Tallahassee, the grounds are surrounded by ancient live oaks where you can do yoga in the gardens, attend a wine tasting in the main house, hear concerts at the carriage house, and lounge beside Tallahassee's oldest pool or under a large wooden pergola that offers plenty of shade.

1600 Miccosukee Rd.
850-877-4202, goodwoodmuseum.org

CREATE ART
AT LEMOYNE ARTS

In 1963, it took four community women leaders to establish the first private organization in Tallahassee that included a non-discriminatory clause in its bylaws. LeMoyne Museum is a fine art gallery created to educate and unite the community through visual arts.

It is a place where the community can participate in the learning, love, and creation of art through classes in painting, stained glass, and drawing, along with open studios and workshops for all ages.

Exhibitions are held in the 1854 antebellum Meginnis-Munroe House, which offers present-day openings for local and regional artists with a permanent collection of works from Karl Zerbe, Nancy Reid Gunn, and Fred Holschuh. Opening exhibit nights offers food, live music and beer from Deep Brewing. The museum also hosts one of the nation's best art shows—Chain of Parks—an Art and Soul Celebration, as well as the must-see annual holiday show featuring handmade ornaments. Before you leave, relax surrounded by fountains in the Helen Lind Sculpture Garden.

125 N Gadsden St.
850-222-8800, lemoyne.org

TIP

Keep an eye out for their Muffins and Mimosas Saturday events with baked goods from Uptown Cafe and live music to enjoy a morning out with the arts.

81

TOUR
THE FLORIDA CAPITOL

At 22 stories high, it is the tallest building in Tallahassee and the third-tallest capitol building in the US. Home to the Florida House of Representatives and the Florida Senate, the state capitol building is in the heart of downtown, only a few steps from the Leon County Courthouse and the Tallahassee City Hall. Enter into the rotunda to appreciate the bronze copy of the Great Seal of the State of Florida mounted on a marble base as you walk down the halls of honor containing the Civil Rights Hall of Fame, the Florida Women's Hall of Fame, the Fallen Firefighters Wall of Honor, and the Florida Artists Hall of Fame. The Heritage Chapel is one of only a few meditative spaces located in a statehouse. Visitors walking through the halls can enjoy professionally painted murals next to middle school student artwork. The most spectacular view in Tallahassee can be seen from the observation deck on the top floor as you walk through a gallery of works by Florida artists.

400 S Monroe St.
850-488-6167, floridacapitol.myflorida.com

LEARN POLITICS
AT FLORIDA HISTORIC CAPITOL MUSEUM

Tallahassee is home to two capitol buildings, a 22-story skyscraper built in 1977 and the old capitol, built in the 1800s and fully restored to its 1902 appearance. The old capitol building now serves as the Florida Historic Capitol Museum where you are encouraged to fully grasp the people and events that impacted the history of the state of Florida and that have shaped it up to the present day. Inside these walls, it is all about politics. Exhibits include restorations of the governor's private office, the cabinet meeting room, and even the room where the Supreme Court of Florida met for ten years. Many of the furnishings in the rooms are original while others have been restored to their original appearance. The most striking piece is found as you look up—a colorful stained glass dome found in between the walls during reconstruction.

400 S Monroe St.
850-487-1902, flhistoriccapitol.gov

EXPLORE AFRICAN AMERICAN HISTORY

AT THE MEEK-EATON BLACK ARCHIVES, RESEARCH CENTER, AND MUSEUM

Thousands of artifacts and over half a million documents dating back to the 1800s help to piece together the story of the African American experience in Florida at the Meek-Eaton Black Archives, Research Center, and Museum, better known as the Black Archives. Located on FAMU's campus, the Black Archives is one of the most extensive museums of African American history in the Southeast. Free of charge to the public, the archives allow you to examine the history of Black participation in sports, Black churches, slavery, and the civil rights movement in the South. Founded in 1976 by James Eaton, a history professor at FAMU, the archives first opened in the historic library of Carnegie Hall on FAMU's campus. As Mr. Eaton said, "African American history is the history of America" and the archives offer a great educational experience through letters, photographs, slave papers, and oral history collections not found elsewhere.

445 Robert and Trudie Perkins Way
850-599-3020, famu.edu/academics/libraries/
meek-eaton-black-archives-research-center-and-museum/index.php

LEARN THE DISTRICTS
OF TALLAHASSEE

Tallahassee has it all! This medium-sized city comprises several varied communities and districts that provide a sense of belonging, unity, and love, not only for what the city used to be but for what it has become and continues to evolve into. Learn what makes each of them unique:

Downtown

Welcome to the capitol building where history continues to take shape in the state. Walk the parks, enjoy the fine restaurants, hotels, and historic mansions, and even visit the Challenger Center.

SOMO (South of Monroe)

Tallahassee's most eclectic, diverse, and artistic district is home to Proof Brewing, the Historic Railroad Square, and First Friday. All this is steps away from FAMU and FSU.

Midtown

Young professionals prefer Midtown for its more trendy and tasteful selection of bars, restaurants, homes, and coffee shops.

Market District

Tallahassee's premier shopping destination has more than 100 boutique-style stores and a wide selection of restaurants.

marketdistricttlh.com

CollegeTown

The party never ends in this section of the city that is home to official Friday Night Block Parties, live music, iconic watering holes, and college students.

fsucollegetown.net

Bannerman/Northside

Tally's newest, most upscale, and fastest-growing district is a city of its own with fine dining, shopping, and the Northtown Getdowns every Friday before a home game at Bannerman Crossings.

bannermancrossings.com

85

EXPERIENCE SOUTHERN LIVING
AT PEBBLE HILL PLANTATION

First bought by Thomas Jefferson in 1825, Pebble Hill Plantation was worked by slaves who planted, then harvested, cotton, sugar cane, corn, and tobacco crops. In 1896, under the ownership of Howard Melville Hanna, the property was turned into a winter home and sporting estate. Grandiosity, abundance, and elegance permeate every awe-inspiring step as you enter the grounds. From the porches of the main house, you can see a carefully tended garden of azaleas and camellias. The giant pool lies empty but it is easy to imagine previous families and friends enjoying a hot summer day in or around the water. Tour the entire property and absorb the sense of peace, stillness, and the passing of history. Pebble Hill Plantation is listed in the National Register of Historic Places.

1251 US Hwy. 319 S, Thomasville, GA
229-226-2344, pebblehill.com

TIP

Bring comfortable shoes and lose yourself while enjoying the sizeable estate. Lay down a blanket, enjoy a picnic, and take it all in on a beautiful spring day. Head toward downtown Thomasville afterward and enjoy some shopping, dining, and local breweries.

SEE THESE PLANTATIONS NEARBY

Sinkola Plantation
101 Sinkola Dr., Thomasville, GA
229-226-4086, sinkola.com/welcome.html

South Eden Plantation
301 Showboat Ln., Thomasville, GA
229-233-8285, southeden.com

SIT IN HISTORY
AT MONTICELLO OPERA HOUSE

Scheduled to be demolished in the 1970s, the Monticello Opera House, formerly known as the Perkins Block, came back to life thanks to the efforts of committed citizens wanting to preserve a piece of American history. Built in 1890 with exceptional acoustics, the opera house had the largest stage in the region at that time. Today, restoration of the building continues even though it is still open to the public for tours and stages plays and performances by local, regional, and national artists. As you enter the building, its history emanates from its floors and walls. The small theater provides intimate opportunities to enjoy artists on a personal level with year-round plays, musicals, dinner theaters, children's theaters, and concerts. The opera house also provides classes for adults who want to participate in the shows, and its beautiful gardens serve as event spaces for weddings and other local events.

185 W Washington St., Monticello
850-997-4242, monticelloperahouse.org

DRIVE THROUGH HISTORY

AT THE TALLAHASSEE AUTOMOBILE MUSEUM

Like any good story, the history of the museum that began as a lifelong passion for collecting and bringing the past into the future while being able to share it with the world can be found at the Tallahassee Automobile Museum. Owner DeVoe Moore started collecting at age nine, and in 1996 he made his collection available to the public. More than 160 automobiles donated by private individuals occupy two floors of a 100,000-square-foot museum building. Admire the beauty, craftsmanship, and style of an extensive collection that includes the 1860 horse-drawn funeral hearse that carried Abraham Lincoln and even the original Batmobiles from the TV series and the movies *Batman Returns* and *Batman Forever*. The museum is more than just cars: Native American artifacts, knives, guns, and Steinway pianos add to the displays. Do not miss this fascinating time-travel experience.

6800 Mahan Dr.
850-942-0137, tacm.com

TASTE GREEK CULTURE
AT THE GREEK FOOD FESTIVAL

What began in the 1980s as a bake sale has grown into the third-largest cultural event in Tallahassee, taking place over two days every November and known as the Greek Food Festival. The event is held at the Holy Mother of God Greek Orthodox Church, where you will also have the opportunity to tour the inside of the church during festival days. The festival is a unique opportunity to immerse fully into Greek life through food and culture. Indulge in its authentic, delicious, and unforgettable food with everyone's favorite gyros, *pastitsio*, *souvlaki*, *tiropita*, and the ever-popular baklava, cooked by volunteers using original recipes brought over from Greece. Shop for jewelry, fun trinkets, and home decor at the Agora and come to life as you watch folk dancing with a traditional live Greek band. Enjoy this authentic taste of Mediterranean life!

1645 Phillips Rd.
850-878-0747, tallahasseegreekfoodfest.wordpress.com

START CONVERSATIONS
AT FSU MUSEUM OF MODERN ART

Museums are places you can enter, get inspired, and see the world differently; so it is with the FSU Museum of Fine Arts (MOFA). With artist talks, opening receptions, ongoing events, and exclusive exhibits, FSU MOFA is a place to celebrate the arts. Work by students, visiting professors, and artists from around the globe adorn the walls of MOFA and allow us to enter their worlds. Experience a peek into the artists' souls, follow their explorations, discover what they love, and even get a glimpse of their darkest places. Engage in a world where you can be free to see the world through someone else's eyes yet simultaneously through your own. Visitors, students, and Tally residents get an opportunity to walk through historical, contemporary, and thought-provoking exhibitions ranging from print work, films, sculptures, and the occasional NFT (non-fungible token). Located on FSU's beautiful campus and with more than 6,000 permanent *objets d'art*, MOFA has an amazing and unforgettable collection.

530 W Call St.
850-644-6836, mofa.fsu.edu

ACHIEVE GREATNESS
AT SOUTHERN SHAKESPEARE COMPANY

Reviving an old tradition while adding a modern flare to it, local actors and Emmy-nominated, Oscar-winning, out-of-town guests bring Shakespeare to life in the capital city. The Southern Shakespeare Company's main festival takes place each Mother's Day weekend, Thursday through Sunday, and offers performances at the Adderley Amphitheater at Cascades Park reminiscent of Shakespeare's time when plays were acted out in outdoor "public" playhouses. Coached by experienced directors from as far away as New York and England, the festival offers quality performances of the caliber seen onstage in larger cities. These are nights to be entertained, educated, and simply mesmerized as you experience Shakespeare 450 years later in this gorgeous venue.

Year-round events surround the festival and, if you are visiting over the summer, perhaps your kids would enjoy a weeklong camp to foster a love of theater while having fun.

These performances make Shakespeare accessible (and lovable) to anyone.

P.O. Box 10050
southernshakespearefestival.org

EXPERIENCE THESE FESTIVALS

FAMU Harambee and Jazz Fest
famu.edu/calendar/index.php?eID=1294

Tallahassee Jazz and Blues Festival
tallahasseemuseum.org/events/tallahassee-jazz-blues-festival

Coolbreeze Art and Smooth Jazz Festival
coolbreezejazzfestival.com

Capital Jazz Fest
capitaljazz.com/fest

Tallahassee PrideFest
tallahasseepride.com

Tallahassee Film Festival
tallahasseefilmfestival.com

Florida Animation Festival
floridaanimationfestival.com

Winter Festival-Parade of Lights
talgov.com/parks/winterevents

Tallahassee Hispanic Theater
tallahasseehispanictheater.org

Cleaver and Cork Food and Wine Festival
cleaverandcorktcc.com/our-events/food-and-wine-festival

Tallahassee Highland Games
tallyhighlandgames.com

Tallahassee Bike Fest
tallybikefest.com

Field Day Music Festival
fielddaytallahassee.com

Wildlife, Heritage, and Outdoors Festival at St. Marks Wildlife Refuge
fws.gov/event/wildlife-heritage-and-outdoors-festival-who

First Friday Festival at Railroad Square
railroadsquare.org

Gifts
Cards
All book club books are 10% off
BLOOD HEAT
MOSTLY DEAD THINGS
THIS POISON HEART
RAINBOW ROWELL
CARRY ON
LUCY FOLEY
THE PARIS APARTMENT
THE PARIS BOOKSELLER
THE FOREST OF VANISHING STARS
KRISTIN HARMEL
Myron L. Rolle
2ND WAY
Myron L. Rolle
2ND WAY
KNOW YOUR WORTH
INCOGNITO
NATIONAL BESTSELLER
THE GUIDE
PETER HELLER
Perfectly PEGASUS
THE GUIDE PETER HELLER
THE GUIDE PETER HELLER
EVENT
books

SHOPPING AND FASHION

BRING HOME A BIKE
FROM A TALLAHASSEE BIKE SHOP

Given our extensive trail system, it's no surprise Tallahassee has plenty of bike shops.

- The Great Bicycle Shop, established in 1971, has over 15 brands and its online portal makes it easy to rent a bike.
- Epic Bikes, located in the Market District, focuses on repairs and builds with a great inventory and weekly scheduled rides for the community.
- David's World Cycle is all about Trek and Bontrager. Service and tune-ups are readily available, and David's provides accessible online guides to help you.
- Joe's Bicycle Shop in Lake Ella offers quality repairs and bikes in the heart of town.
- Bicycle House Tallahassee is the only nonprofit bike shop committed to serving those in need. An apprentice program, workshops, and youth camps are available.
- Hubs and Hops at the Hub at Feathered Oaks is the only bike shop located across the Miccosukee Greenway that offers sales, rentals, and tune-ups with a taproom next door.

You simply can't leave Tally without a bike!

The Great Bicycle Shop
1909 Thomasville Rd.
850-224-7461, gbs.bike

Epic Bikes
1410 Market St.
850-942-2453, epicbikeshop.com

David's World Cycle
2784 Capital Circle NE
850-422-1075, trekbikes.com/us/en_us/retail/tallahassee/?y_source=1_NDA0ODE2MTQtNzE1LWxvY2F0aW9uLndlYnNpdGU%3D

Joe's Bicycle Shop
1637 N Monroe St.
850-222-3855, joes-bicycle-shop.business.site

Bicycle House Tallahassee
458 FAMU Way
850-350-8000, bicyclehouse.org

The Hub at Feather Oaks
6500 Miccosukee Rd.
850-559-0424, thehubatfeatheroaks.com

FEED YOUR SOUL
AT HEARTH AND SOUL

A unique, welcoming, and luxurious shopping experience awaits at Hearth and Soul. Step into the retail home, vision, and dream of Susie Busch-Transou, where everything is carefully selected, from local artisan goods to modern brands and exclusive commodities. Hearth and Soul is beautifully designed as a home. As you walk into the foyer, you will marvel at the homey spaces: mudroom, his and her closets, kitchen, family room, library, and even a patio. Everything you see is available for purchase, including the table showcasing the jewelry, the mirror and artwork on the walls, and the chandeliers. It's a place where you can visualize how an item would fit into your home. Frequent events are hosted at Hearth and Soul, including yoga classes and music on the patio, book signings, art shows, happy hours, and fundraising events.

1410 Market St., Ste. D1
850-894-7685, hearthandsoul.com

TIP

Susie has expanded Hearth and Soul into Austin, Texas, and St. Louis, Missouri.

UP YOUR FASHION GAME
AT GYPSY ROSE BOUTIQUE

Love of fashion, retail, and luxury motivated the founding of Gypsy Rose Boutique. After working with Chanel and Mac Cosmetics, Maria Raquel established Gypsy Rose in 2015 out of a burning love for retail. With two locations in Tallahassee, one in the Market District and the other one in Bannerman Crossings, Gypsy Rose Boutique has become a little gem in the city for women who want to feel and look their best. Offering a unique selection of fashion, Gypsy's friendly and helpful team will make you feel comfortable with your purchase every step of the way. Karlie Ditsy, Free People, and Fidelity are a few of the brands carried by Gypsy Rose. Featuring tops, bottoms, dresses, shoes, jewelry, and even candles, you are sure to find something you will love at Gypsy Rose Boutique.

1350 Market St., Ste. 104
850-765-5595

3421 Bannerman Rd., Ste. 101
850-727-4437, gypsyroseapparel.com

TIP

Gypsy Rose's Market Square location provides the perfect opportunity to shop the Market District stores. Enjoy breakfast at Jeri's Love on a Plate, lunch at Gordos or Momos Pizza, or even the occasional sinful pastry at Tasty Pastry.

LOVE THE OUTDOORS
AT REI

It may not be a local store, yet this nationwide retailer found a home in our beloved Tallahassee. On opening weekend, locals were heard to exclaim, “We finally got an REI!” Located in the Market District, we like to think that REI got lucky when it opened its doors in Tallahassee in November of 2022. REI is the perfect store for a city soon to be blessed with 100 parks, over 70 miles of trails, and the special nickname of “Trailahassee.” Our capital city is all about being outdoors, and whether you are a novice, intermediate adventure seeker, or intense multiday explorer, REI offers a great selection of gear and clothing for all outdoor lovers. Whether you are into camping, hiking, running, cycling, climbing, or even outdoor yoga, REI has what you need. Walk in, consult with REI’s knowledgeable salespeople, and get the gear you need to enjoy the outside world.

1415 Timberlane Rd., Ste. 201
850-201-1938, rei.com/stores/tallahassee

95

STROLL DOWNTOWN
IN THOMASVILLE, GEORGIA

Less than 45 minutes away from Tallahassee, not far from the Florida–Georgia border, you will find the small, charming, and historical town of Thomasville, Georgia. Known as Georgia's Rose City, downtown Thomasville provides a fabulous escape and the opportunity to experience a true, distinguished, and walkable southern town. Downtown Thomasville thrives with art galleries, antique shops, furniture stores, boutiques, and a wide array of amazing restaurants. Listen to live music at Hubs and Hops, a unique blend of bike shop and taproom. Visit Thomasville's first-ever 1861 Distillery and enjoy its first craft brewing company at T'Velo Brewing while enjoying their great outdoor patio. Starting in March, the city comes alive on first Fridays with free concerts at the Ritz Amphitheater, and in December, Victorian Christmas is a must.

144 E Jackson St., Thomasville, GA
229-227-7020, thomasvillega.com/downtown-thomasville

TIP

On your way back to Tallahassee, head over to Fish Camp and enjoy live music, drinks, and food by the water.

DISCOVER THESE RESTAURANTS IN THOMASVILLE

Sass
420 W Jackson St., Thomasville, GA
229-236-6006, sassthomasville.com

Liam's Restaurant
113 E Jackson St., Thomasville, GA
229-226-9944, liamsthomasville.com

Jonah's Fish and Grits
109 E Jackson St., Thomasville, GA
229-226-0508, jonahsfish.com

Chop House on the Bricks
123 N Broad St., Thomasville, GA
229-236-2696, chophouseonthebricks.com

St. James Restaurant
1145 W Jackson St., Thomasville GA
229-221-3056, stjamesthomasville.com

96

SHOP 'TIL YOU DROP
AT TALLAHASSEE'S BOUTIQUES

Tallahassee is home to a unique selection of shops and boutiques scattered throughout the city. Each has a unique appeal; they provide a personalized experience coupled with exclusive clothing items made with high-quality materials to encourage your love for fashion for years to come.

Divas and Devils House of Style

Romantic, edgy, and even wildflower women with an obsession for elegant vintage designer clothes can all find their personal, inspiring, and timeless style at Divas and Devils.

1300 N Monroe St.
850-580-6662, divasanddevils.com

Lobos Boutique

A mom-and-daughter team with a dream to keep up with the trends. Casual, comfortable, and trendy pieces for women who want to look good.

3425 Bannerman Rd., #101
850-264-6889, lobosboutiquetally.com

Ooh La La

Fun clothes, good prices, and edgy pieces for women who want to have a good time can be found at Ooh La La.

699 W Gaines St.
850-583-8980, instagram.com/oohlalatallyboutique/?hl=en

Narcissus

It's time to dress up, feel gorgeous, and head to the home of fashion for the past 30 years in Tallahassee. Luxury, sophistication, and style come together at Narcissus.

1408 Timberlane Rd.
850-668-4807, narcissusstyle.com

Sparkle

A desire for affordably priced fashion chosen by a friendly team in a store that has it all will lead you to Sparkle.

2627 Capital Cir. NE
850-567-1805, sparkletallahassee.com

Lady Luck Boutique

Exclusive clothing, accessories, and handbags that create trends great for every occasion can be found at Lady Luck Boutique.

1533 S Monroe St.
llbladyluck.com

97

SURROUND YOURSELF WITH BEAUTY
AT TALLAHASSEE NURSERIES

It's not just a place to purchase flowers, citrus, herbs, or trees, but rather it is where you come to experience exquisite beauty, the sound of the birds in the middle of the city, and the calming and delightful splash of the water fountains. Walk through over 80 years of excellent service at Tallahassee Nurseries. What started as a small five-acre farm that sold produce, azaleas, and camellias has become an 11-acre oasis for plant lovers, casual shoppers, or those who just need a tranquil place to get away. Tallahassee Nurseries is a full-service nursery with a flower and gift shop, garden center, and greenhouse. They are fully connected to the community and host many events year-round like Garden Yoga, live music, and the pre-Christmas Artisans in the Garden sale every November where more than 50 local artists display pieces they wish to sell dispersed throughout one of the most beautiful gardens in the capital city.

2911 Thomasville Rd.
850-385-2162, tallahasseenurseries.com

FIND YOUR STYLE
AT TALLY'S BEST MEN'S SHOP

Nic's Toggery

Opened by a master tailor in 1950, Nic's Toggery has been a staple of sartorial class, elegance, and nobility in Tallahassee for the southeast region. Hand-selected to fit your taste and lifestyle, these southern influencers will guarantee a personal experience in the comfort of your home, by private appointment, through special events, or as a casual walk-in. With three locations in the capital city, it is time for men to think differently about shopping.

212 S Monroe St.
850-222-0687

1455 Market St.
850-893-9599

1475 Market St.
850-385-6866

nicstoggery.com

Southern Compass Outfitters

A more casual, laid back, and modern men's clothing store in the heart of Midtown has been dressing our men for 10 years. Walk in, shop online, or schedule a private appointment and choose from a wide selection of brands like Vuori, Red Hills Clothing Co., Northern Tail, and Fish Hippie, among many others. Come see what it is like to be treated like family the moment you walk in.

1817 Thomasville Rd., Ste. 610
850-765-7172, southerncompassoutfitters.com

99

REDISCOVER THE PAST
AT TALLAHASSEE'S ANTIQUES SHOPS

Every piece has a story and often the item holds a secret waiting to be discovered. Welcome to Tallahassee's antiques shops. It's time to dig through the past, find hidden treasures, and bring it all back to life. Tallahassee is home to a series of antique shops that are sure to captivate you.

Talquin Trading Co.

Named after the reservoir that separates Tallahassee and Quincy, Talquin is not your typical antiques and collectibles store. Rare and unusual items can often be found here, and if they don't have exactly what you are looking for, the folks at Talquin will find it for you. After 10 years in the nearby town of Havana, the Railroad Square Art District is now home to Talquin Trading Co.

629 Industrial Dr.
850-591-7736, facebook.com/talquintradingco

Memory Lane Antiques

This place has all the vintage and antique treasures you want for your home or for that special antique-loving friend of yours: an incomparable collection of art, glass, pottery, furniture, and even jewelry in a museum-like setting that allows you to buy it and take it home if you want. Enjoy the beauty of time at Memory Lane Antiques.

1425 N Monroe St.
850-577-1045, memorylanetallahasseeantiques.com

Canopy Road Antiques

One-of-a-kind, elegant, and beautiful costume jewelry, art, glassware, and books are waiting for you in a store that specializes in estates. Opened by antique dealers Ron and Marcia, they share their love for antiques at Canopy Road Antiques.

2744 Capital Cir. NE
850-523-0843, facebook.com/canopyroadsantiques

Bob's Vintage and Antiques

Antique furniture and rare vintage pieces to decorate your home can be found at Bob's Vintage and Antiques.

3510 N Monroe St.
850-765-2197, bobs-vintage-and-antiques.business.site

100

GET READY FOR THE GAME

AT GARNET AND GOLD

Tallahassee is known as a college town where the Seminoles of Florida State University (FSU), one of the largest public universities in the country, glow in garnet and gold. Down the road, the Rattlers of Florida Agricultural and Mechanical University (FAMU), the only historically Black university in Florida's state system, show off their orange and green. Hats, hoodies, T-shirts, shoes, socks, ties—you name it—anywhere you turn you will see people sporting and supporting their preferred team's colors. Although most stores sell FSU and FAMU gear, there are a few must-go places to get your premier apparel and merchandise. Garnet and Gold has been serving Tallahassee and every loyal Seminole for over 35 years. With four locations in the capital city, you are sure to find what you need. For your Rattler gear, step inside the apparel and spirit shop at the FAMU bookstore.

It's time to show your spirit by sporting the right gear!

Garnet and Gold–Flagship Store
1504 Governor's Square Blvd.
850-942-2221
garnetandgold.com

Florida A&M University
Official Bookstore
601 Robert and Trudie Perkins Way
famu.bncollege.com

TIP

On game weekends, many vendors will have pop-up shops near campus for your school-spirit gear!

GET MORE SEMINOLES GEAR

Alumni Hall
1817 Thomasville Rd., #250
850-425-1006, alumnihall.com/florida-state-seminoles

Bill's Bookstore
111 S Copeland St.
850-224-3178, bkstr.com/billsbookstore/home

Barefoot Campus Outfitter
619 S Woodward Ave., #104
850-403-3752, barefootcampusoutfitter.com/
florida-state

PALACE SALOON
WHERE EVERY DAY IS GAME DAY
TALLAHASSEE, FL.
PALACE
SALOON
5K !
DO WORK

SUGGESTED ITINERARIES

FAMILY FRIENDLY

THE GREAT OUTDOORS

EYE FOR BEAUTY

SPORTS FANS

FOODIES

DAY TRIPS

SHOPPERS

HISTORY LOVERS

ACTIVITIES
BY SEASON

Following are some of my top season-specific recommendations. Also check out the list of annual festivals on page 115 in case you're lucky enough to be in Tallahassee to enjoy those as well.

SPRING

Stroll through the Art at LeMoyne's Chain of Parks Art Festival, 38

Experience the Joy at Word of South, 36

Celebrate our Capital's History at Springtime Tallahassee, 40

Get Hooked at the National High Magnetic Field Laboratory, 95

Achieve Greatness at Southern Shakespeare Company, 114

Listen to the Music at Tallahassee Symphony Orchestra, 43

SUMMER

Achieve Greatness at Southern Shakespeare Company, 114

See Old Florida at Edward Ball Wakulla Springs State Park, 69

Fish at the St. Marks River, 60

Bike, Hike, and Horseback Ride the Trails at J.R. Alford Greenway, 70

Kayak or Paddleboard the Wakulla River, 85

Find the Big Blue at Wacissa River, 62

FALL

WINTER

INDEX